THE POETRY TRIALS

THE SOUTH WEST

Edited by Jenni Bannister

First published in Great Britain in 2016 by:

Young**Writers**

Remus House
Coltsfoot Drive
Peterborough
PE2 9BF
Telephone: 01733 890066
Website: www.youngwriters.co.uk

FOREWORD

Welcome, Reader!

For Young Writers' latest competition, *The Poetry Trials*, we gave secondary school students nationwide the challenge of writing a poem. They were given the option of choosing a restrictive poetic technique, or to choose any poetic style of their choice. They rose to the challenge magnificently, with young writers up and down the country displaying their poetic flair.

We chose poems for publication based on style, expression, imagination and technical skill. The result is this entertaining collection full of diverse and imaginative poetry, which is also a delightful keepsake to look back on in years to come.

Here at Young Writers our aim is to encourage creativity in the next generation and to inspire a love of the written word, so it's great to get such an amazing response, with some absolutely fantastic poems. It made choosing the winners extremely difficult, so well done to *Poppy Wakefield* who has been chosen as the best in this book. Their poem will go into a shortlist from which the top 5 poets will be selected to compete for the ultimate Poetry Trials prize.

I'd like to congratulate all the young poets in *The Poetry Trials – The South West –* I hope this inspires them to continue with their creative writing.

Jenni Bannister

Editorial Manager

A POEM IS JUST THE BEGINNING...

CONTENTS

Hele's School, Plymouth

Holsworthy Community College, Holsworthy

Penrice Academy, St Austell

Redruth School, Redruth

St Bede's Catholic College, Bristol

St Mary's School, Shaftesbury

Stanchester Academy, Stoke-Sub-Hamdon

Voyage Learning Campus – Weston, Oldmixon

THE POEMS

AEROPLANE CLOUDS

I see you, and I understand,
Why people lie down to sleep,
In the obtuse and splendid hope,
That they will wake,
And see the orange sun.

The timer is set,
For our glorious denouncement,
But with fleeting heart beats,
You steady my thoughts,
And shake my sight.

When the old record player,
You placed upon the table,
Turns and turns and stops,
It cuts our melody short,
And I linger in the lullaby.

So close your dusty eyes,
Look past the splinters,
And in this cloying reverie,
Picture cold mornings,
And scalding coffee cups.

And when the wistful mist creeps in,
Go not to the yellow street lights,
But look up into the sky
And see my smile in the aeroplane clouds.

Hannah Born

POETICALLY JUDGED

Someone asked me
'Why are you depressed?'
I answered truthfully and said . . .

Coz of all this s**t
All these names, all these games
They all just get to me.

Because . . .
You can never go round a corner and not get judged,
Because you judge me, and I judge you,
You're as bad as me, and I'm as bad as you,
So why are we judging each other?
Because . . . it's not about place or game,
It's about our face and our game.

Whether we drive a car or catch a bus,
Either one, we should be defined as us,
We all say 'treat people equally' but we don't,
We don't, not at all,
All these people on benefits are considered poor,
And people over a certain wage are considered rich,
I doubt a good waged rich man will hitch because he's scared,
Scared of the fact he might be downgraded for being more down to earth.

But isn't that wrong,
Judging someone who just wants to be human,
Someone who just wants to be free from hate,
Someone who just wants to have love in his heart,
Someone who wants to try something new,
But he's just someone who won't be accepted,
That's why he deliberately misses the chance to hitch,
Because he won't be accepted,
He will be considered a poor man with minimum wage,
He will be considered a joke,
Because he's putting his faith in strangers,
Because he's at risk of so many dangers,
From so many strangers.

It all comes down to one thing though,
Trying to be human . . .
But who really is human?
Because I don't know,
And I doubt you or any man would either.

So stop judging me,
And I'll stop judging you.

So I ask you . . .
Why are you judging that person by one look?
Why are you so hateful?
What's made you so ungrateful?
Because this isn't you, at least not the human you,
So stop with the act, and be yourself,
Not what your peers want you to be.

Don't judge by names, or games, or places, or faces
Colour or background or experience,
Judge from the heart and the energy you feel,
Not by the old scars that don't seem to heal,
Those are scars from their past!
And those people are strong enough to be here now,
And bear that old ripped skin,
That may make your blood boil,
Or blood go thin.
Whichever one it still makes them human,
So ask about the markings of treachery on their wrist,
The story they tell might end with an unforgivable twist,
But at least the story's been told,
And their conscience has nothing to hold.

So don't let others get depressed like me,
Don't let them over think about all this s**t,
All of these names and all of these f****** games,
Don't let it get to them,
Because it's just too late for me.

'Treat others how you wish to be treated'
That's all I have to say that's in my heart that has to be said.

Natalie Neame (16)

MOTHER NATURE

One minute stars across the sky
Like little diamonds shining
Is it Mother Nature?

The sun is as fierce as fire
It shocks you when you see it
Is it Mother Nature?

The trees are giants
Swiftly blowing in the calm breeze
They wave to you
Sometimes fast
Sometimes slow
Is it Mother Nature?

The sea gently laps
Upon the rocks
Like a cat drinking milk
Is it Mother Nature?

The clouds like soft bits of meringue
Floating above humanity
Is it Mother Nature?

Little birds sit there and chirp happily
They are little squeakers in toys
Is it Mother Nature?

Tiny insects crawl beneath your feet
They are pieces of dirt
Blowing in the cooling breeze
Is it Mother Nature?

Fish are like curtains
Waving in the wind
Elegantly swishing through the water
is it Mother Nature?

Birds fly through the air
Like an arrow in the war
Is it Mother Nature?

Storms brew above for hours
Slowly lingering in the sky
Until finally they explode
Is it Mother Nature?

Ben Tilley

MAN OF THE MOON

The mountains, they have cried a mournful cry
As the man of the night wanders by

His hair of youthful silver
Forever puzzles them
His eyes of iridescent life
That wind through the skies
Although he never puzzles me
I have seen him

I have looked into the lake below
Like a city centre full of desires, deceit and desperation
The lake will forever smile up at you
As long as you smile down at it

I have wandered the skies
Throughout the blissful night
My time is slowly rocket speeding away
So now I lie on clouds of silk
My time is up, my time is gone

So I shall send one more glance
To the world below
The rivers of sapphires
The lake of topaz
And I shall see myself
With my silver hair.

Clarice Wyatt (12)

NORTH AND SOUTH

As her eyes lurched towards mine like bent keys trying to find the lock
and our enchained fingers made a highway, a link road between us,
I told the Northern Lights to be silent
because I wanted her to have her heart attack in peace.

Last winter I swam to her through the velocity of the ice
and I cut my ankles on shackles and I did it twice.
Over the icebergs I climbed to reach her,
through the high-pitched boulevards in the whistle of the night.
When I got to her she was dead but I brought her back to life.

She lived in a quiet town on the island on the other side.
It was the place that they put on postcards,
drenched in glitter, bright, crystallised,
but to her and the others who lived there: it was dark.

The lights had gone and I felt her statin-infused blood pulp against the pipes under her skin,
so I told her 'thank you' and she told me 'goodbye',
but we still held each other like North and South
and we wept like flightless birds.

- that is how I feel when I hold her ashes in my hand.

Lils James

NEPHEW

If my nephew could speak this is what he'd say

Can you guess it?

Comforting and calming
Always by my side
When my cries are alarming
You never try to hide

You make me giggle
You take my pain away
Even when I wriggle
You tend to stay

You put up with tears
You put up with spit
You disperse my fears
You're constantly bit!

You're the first resort made by Mummy
When I cry and she knows not what to do
She consoles me by saying I'm a dummy
Funny thing is you are one too!

Sam Reeves (16)

MUSIC

Phone on
Earphones in
Play pressed
Pause untouched
Volume up
Outside world closed off
My world opened up

Phone dead
Earphones out
Play gone
Pause not needed
No volume control
Outside world is my only world
My world is gone!

Music takes me to my home
No music, no home
No battery, no phone
No music to take me to my home.

Charlotte Brumpton (14)

CHAMELEON

I'm chameleon
Stuck here in this zoo prison
With ugly people
I am so lonely
I always beg to be free
It never happens
No flies to munch on
Nothing for me to run from
Why do I just sit?
My skin changing shades
But no reason why I should
Why do I do that?
My long tail just hangs
Full of sadness and anger
I wish to be free
Soon I will escape
Heading for my family
So soon I'll be free.

Thomas Owen (14)

LIFE

We love and we lose, we make decisions, then we choose.
We cry, we laugh, we all go through something that's hard.
We make mistakes to learn again, mine started at ten.
We fall in love to get our heart broken, we get used like a single token.
We all hold memories that we will never go, even if they didn't show.
We all have that one person, we latch onto the one person we attach to.
We all have our struggles, at one point we all sink in the dark puddles.
Day to day still make the same mistake and all we did was try to give and never take.

Leanne Williams (16)
Atkinson Secure School And Home, Exeter

WISHING

When life throws you lemons
You make lemonade
But when life throws you painful memories
You just wish they went away
Even though they scar you
And leave a mark
You wish you could press rewind
And go back to the start
When everything was fine
And everyone was glad
When we were a family
But I guess it didn't last
Because if everything was alright
And I was fine
Then I wouldn't be here
Wishing all the time

Amirah Irani (15)
Atkinson Secure School And Home, Exeter

THE SUN

If it could speak it would say,
'I let you know when it is day.
I help the plants and crops grow.
I keep you warm through the day.
When I leave the moon will show.
Then I come back
The next day.
And again I will go.
Sometimes the clouds
Allow me to hide.
But when they pass I will start to shine.'

Jay Cooper (14)
Atkinson Secure School And Home, Exeter

REALISTIC GAMING

I got home from the dreadful, mind-boggling school.
I whipped out my controller and I was going to play my favourite game:
Plants vs Zombies Garden Warfare.
I logged in with a smile and a beating heart.
I played as a chomper, the leaves dangling from the back of his purple spotty neck – he can burrow underground like a hungry mole.
His dagger-sharp teeth aligning around his mouth like stars that are glinting.
He gobbles up zombies like the Bermuda Triangle gobbles planes.
I felt like I was in the game, the sweat pouring down my neck the pixelated squares guided me to victory's path.
I levelled up one after another. As time passed the chomper grew and grew.
Until he was the king of the server.
A zombie appeared, it was the All-Star.
The two kings clashed as the teeth of the chomper bit the metal golf club *'shing'* the club went as it scraped across the teeth.
'You shall fall upon the might of the All-Star,' said the All-Star.
The chomper grinned knowing his meal was at hand.
Zing, zing, chomp – the All-Star was gobbled up.

Dillon Vine (13)
Caradon Short Stay School, Liskeard

THE RACE

The smell of the petrol
The engine roar
Makes me tremble but wanting more
Wind in my face cheers from the crowd
I can't believe it, I feel so proud
The tyres screech
We cross the line
Everybody screaming
It's riot time.

Liam Smith (13)
Caradon Short Stay School, Liskeard

SPARKLERS

Bright; dazzling
Shining up above
Smiling, excited and cheerful
Fireworks.

Zara Leanne Foster (15)
Caradon Short Stay School, Liskeard

FIREWORKS

Glowing flame in the sky
Where it dazzles in my eyes
Explodes in the night
Like bright glitter.

Morgan Pengelly (12)
Caradon Short Stay School, Liskeard

STORM

Rain penetrates silence,
Always keeps to the beat.
Drops create puddles.

Thunder is always too late,
Grumbling to the next stop.
Giants are clapping.

Calm before the storm.
The wind howls like a werewolf.
Trees bend down in awe.

Flash!
It's there, but gone.
Lightning forks through the dark sky.
White, bright light flashes.

Ruby Campbell-Whelan (11)
Cotham School, Bristol

LIGHT

I was once a lonely neighbour
As quiet as can be.
When all of a sudden
There was a bright light glowing next to me.

It had two eyes and a mouth
And it said to me
To come explore the world
With him until I'm sixteen.

So he brought me to his house
To meet this family
When unfortunately
It was quarter past three.

So I waved goodbye,
Gave him a kiss.
Then he told me to make a wish.

Then I thought to myself
'What shall I do?
I know I wish you could come with me too.'

But I knew that he wouldn't come there.
So I said, 'Who are you?'
Then got sent back home.

So I curled up
Into my new bed
And there was a note.
It had my name on it.
I opened it and it said:
'My name is Snowy the Shooting Star
And I'll always be there
To give you light'.

Avea Archer
Cotham School, Bristol

LIGHT

On Sunday I went caving.
The rocks were really tight.
I couldn't see my hands or feet.
I was praying for some light.

I was stuck between the rocks,
And my heart began to race.
I hated being in the dark.
There was a panic on my face.

The noise was deadly silent.
I couldn't hear a thing.
I'm incredibly scared at this moment.
I wish my phone would ring.

I couldn't get a signal.
So I can't phone a friend.
Even if I could see my texts,
They wouldn't be able to send.

It's dark in here and very cold.
It's wet and even damp.
I pray for light to help me see.
The way back to my camp.

I'm now becoming hungry.
I want some food or drink.
I really wish for some light,
Because that would help me think.

What's that ahead?
I think I see a light.
I begin to wander closer,
And it's getting rather bright.

At last I think I might be safe.
Maybe I'll escape.
Or is it my imagination.
I'm really lacking faith.

I've been here for several hours,
And I really want to go,
But sometimes I think to myself,

I'm stuck here. Oh no!

It's very late on Sunday,
And I need to get some sleep.
I don't know what time it is.
I really could just weep.

I can't go on for much longer.
I'm really feeling sick.
I need to get out fast.
Where's the light switch to flick?

There's something up ahead.
It really is for real.
I'm sure I'm seeing something bright.
I'm getting a warm feel.

It's definitely light I see.
I know the way out.
I'm feeling much happier.
I may just have to shout.

'Ahoy!' I cry. 'Yippee, hooray!'
I'm happy to see the light.
It makes no sense to many people,
But this brings me much delight.

Home at last. What a relief.
I'm so glad to see the sun.
'Cause stuck in the dark, scared and wet
Is certainly no fun!

Alfie Luing
Cotham School, Bristol

THE CITY SKY

Walk up the twisting stairs,
Press fingers to the cold,
And watch the scene,
Behind the glass,
Unfold.

The endless, ceaseless,
Moving clouds,
Glide,
Rapidly across the sky,
Falling,
Like a midnight blanket,
Over the city,
And in the wake of darkness
Comes,
A stream of flickering lights,
Appearing quickly,
One after the other,
As if a nimble hand had lit them.

Push against the window,
Lean out and feel,
The painted picture become
Real,
Breathe deeply,
Smell the city air,
Reach,
And see if you can catch,
The night.

The distant,
Constant,
Roar of traffic,
A sky tinged with urban warmth and
Punctured,
With silver stars,
A sleepy moon.

But below the city is very much,
Alive,
Each flickering light becomes a story,

Illuminated by
A single candle,
Or a hundred bulbs,
A girl dancing in a sea of stars.

And all this is snatched up by the wind,
Caught captive on the breeze,
Left vulnerable,
With dreams and hopes,
Under the pin-prick lights,
And the endless,
Ceaseless,
Moving clouds.

Ella Rose Bragonier (14)
Cotham School, Bristol

LIGHT

When you're inside your bed hearing squeaking and creaking,
Of loose floorboards and doors hanging off hinges,
All you want is light to guide you out of the horror of night,
You were told that monsters were only in stories,
By mothers trying to calm your ghostly theories,
Of figures that end up being old scarves,
Or toys that you thought to be strange body parts,
I know that by 11 I shouldn't believe in these things,
But I cannot stop myself having these strings,
Of thoughts that seem to take over my mind,
And childhood imaginings often maligned,
By parents who forgot at the age of 18,
What darkness they have really seen,
Inside their minds when they were our age,
When they were at that visionary stage,
In bed like I am right now,
Being swallowed up by an ominous cloud,
So all I want is some beautiful light,
To guide me out of this treacherous night.

Lola English
Cotham School, Bristol

THE COLOUR OF LIGHT

A blazing light in the midst of a black winter's evening,
An opening in a tangle of darkness.
The eyes of an invisible beast
Crawl slowly across the sky.
And yet something stirs unheard and unseen,
Yet so visible in the fading light of day:
The light of hopes so clear and bright
Illuminates sad faces of regret.

A new birth so new and happy,
No sadness nor despair -
So pure.
So new.
No regrets, no
Desperate wishes.
Only the colours of the light falling softly on the eyes.
Greeting with a drifting hello.

The colours of light brighten
New space in a tangle of memory:
The ability to change,
To hope.
Even when the sky is dark and clouds
Pour their way over the sky,
The colour of light is still there:
A blazing light in the midst of a black winter's evening.

Sophie Rebecca Jones (12)
Cotham School, Bristol

STARLIGHT

When the sun goes to sleep
When the sky falls to night
And the crickets begin to sing
You sparkle like sequins
You twinkle like gems
You shine from star to eye

When it's as black as night
Starlight, you brighten my night

Ganymede pours water into the sky
As Pegasus flies so high
The Hydra slithers
Lupus howls
And Pavo struts in the dark

When it's as black as night
Starlight, you brighten my night

Like a wizard's cloak there's magic inside
When you shoot through the black mist
People whisper their wishes

When it's as black as night
Starlight, you brighten my night.

Nina Fae Fae Brockis (12)
Cotham School, Bristol

LIGHT BEAM

It glistens, it gleams,
It skips across the water in a summer's dream.
Jumping and hopping from window to window,
This mesmerising magic will creep up onto your pillow.
But, at night, it softens to a silvery glow,
Then lights up the houses and streets below.
All day it dances across the floor causing shadows to be seen,
Moving all the time, it's a beautiful light beam.

Mackenzie Westlake
Cotham School, Bristol

THE BEAUTIFUL MOON

I open the curtains
And what do I see?
A beautiful light
Shining on me.

Where is it coming from?
So late at night!
When I'm in bed?
It doesn't seem right!

It's shining on my covers
Making them so bright
I don't understand.
What is that light?

From behind a cloud
Out it is creeping
Shining so brightly
While everyone is sleeping.

It's getting even brighter.
Now I can see
It's the beautiful moon
Shining on me.

Morgan Bagnall
Cotham School, Bristol

THE TORCH LIGHT

I gave you a torchlight.
It should light your way through the dark,
Cold night.
It will save you from
The mysterious monsters.
It will shine your way.

We will use it in our adventures.
It will help you fight the night.

Pablo Romero (11)
Cotham School, Bristol

SEASONS LIGHT

The light in spring is exciting and new,
Shimmering rays are there to comfort you.
Sun peeking shyly through the new leaves.
Beautifully through the branches it weaves.

Magically, the summer sun shines all day.
Unfortunately, it never seems to stay
When it rains but the sun is still bright
It creates an arch of different coloured light.

As the leaves go red and the sun is down
The sun makes light a splendid golden brown.
In the morn, whilst the leaves fall,
The light fades out into a misty ball.

When the sun does shine it'll have a milky hue,
Cracks in the clouds they come beaming through.
In the winter the light is often poor,
But this can make us feel cosy when we're not sure.

Fraser Royston
Cotham School, Bristol

THE LIGHT FADES

The exploding shrapnel littered the field
As an eruption of light shines upon a broken past,
Then falls and is shattered.

The light begins to fade
As a broken 'peace' of the past lumbers to a halt;
Lying upon the ground,
The shattered piece of history begins
To slowly and painfully become still.

The light fades as a broken soul
Disappears into the everlasting darkness of war
That is always here.
But light is triumphant!

Daniel Everington
Cotham School, Bristol

THE LIGHT

The rays slice through the air.
The flashes that blind my eyes.
The light that brightens my heart
And shrouds out the dark.

The shine is everywhere.
The brightness that paints the skies.
The glow that enlightens me
And shatters the dark.

The sparkle that goes here and there.
The dazzle that jumps and flies.
The blaze that makes me happy
And crushes the dark.

The darkness is nowhere.
The light is everywhere.
My soul is enlightened
And guarded from the dark.

Peter Medus
Cotham School, Bristol

LIGHT

From the flickering lamps in the night
to the immense skyscrapers towering over the city,
they all create light.
When the sun comes over the horizon,
when birds are chattering in the morning light,
people start coming out.
Children playing early in the park – screaming and shouting.
Angry neighbours shaking their fists at the noisy children.
A spectrum of colours: red, to green, to indigo.
It helps us see.
It destroys shadows.
Light is a wonderful thing.

Lucas Herbert Holik (11)
Cotham School, Bristol

THE DARKNESS AND THE LIGHT

Darkness filled the world,
no light to extinguish the gloom.
Suddenly, stars, sun and crescent moon
descended to ward off the oncoming doom.
Their light was mesmerising,
and had a heavenly glow.
Darkness dropped to the lowest of the low,
as light flooded the world's every corner.
As for the Leader of Dark,
this would have torn her,
had it not been for the night sky
that had survived.
Nowadays Light and Night share the world half and half,
But in winter or summer,
they overstay.
So that's why in winter the nights are longer,
And for the summer the sun strives stronger.

Eleni Vargas Lewis (11)
Cotham School, Bristol

LIGHT

When the rays shift,
Countless trembling
For raindrops on birch twigs;
They fade to nothing
In the subtle morning brightness,
Until night falls
Encasing the shining tree
In utter darkness.
When a breeze blows
Through grasses or branches
Light touches the heart.
There are no witnesses
Other than the light.

Terry Bickerton (11)
Cotham School, Bristol

23

LIGHT

Light, light burning bright
In the middle of the night.
Noises, noises everywhere,
Giving me a great, big scare.
Is it a burglar?
Should I peep?
Maybe I'll go back to sleep.
Light, light, annoying light,
Giving me a blurry sight.
Who is coming in my room?
Perhaps it's a witch on her broom.
I rub my eyes then to find
My sister hauling up the blind,
'Get up, get up, you lazy toad!
Your friends are waiting on Gloucester Road.'
Now I'm up, oh I wish I could be
back in be in a deep, deep sleep.

Sam Swayne (11)
Cotham School, Bristol

LIGHT

Light gushes down from above the canopy
Illuminating objects so you don't trip haphazardly.
A butterfly of light comes down and lands on your balcony
Filtering down from nothingness; made out of alchemy.
Light falls from Heaven, way up above
Free to go anywhere, free as a dove.
It keeps your body warm as a glove.

Light rains down on Earth with its heavenly splendour
And all things it touches brighter it shall render.
Light is for everyone and completely free,
Because it touches everything that you see.

Rufus Iles
Cotham School, Bristol

LIGHT

Firelight consumes
While scented candles perfume.

The starlight twinkles
But moonlight is our symbol.

Sunlight is food for food
But reflective rain is life
And then there's the cuttlefish,
The luminescent cuttlefish.
They rule the seas with their enchanting rays
And spectacular looks.

Furthermore, you mustn't forget the jellyfish,
The photonic jellyfish.
They roam the seas
With their radiant beams
Overpowering all of its enemies.

Tiye Thomas-Smith (12)
Cotham School, Bristol

LIGHT

There is nothing we can see
Alone in the dark
Tripping and falling
Walking blindly as if in a maze.
We are lost.

And then suddenly,
Light.
A flicker of flames
A roaring fire
Shadows dancing across the walls.

Guiding us through a never-ending darkness
Glowing brightly in the dark
Lighting up the way.

Naomi Wood (12)
Cotham School, Bristol

36 DEGREES IN THE SHADE

The scorching sun raged like a bear.
A thin layer of sunlight glittered on the rippling harbour.
The cacophony of noises merged together, creating a white noise.
Staring in amazement at the glorious river, I was unaware that my chocolate ice cream
was dripping down my hand.
I plodded on into the shade.
My cherry-red face finally began to cool.
The boats bobbed and bounced over the elegantly curling water,
the rays of light reflecting into my eyes.
I found an old willow tree and lay down under the small, thin, intertwining branches.
I listened to the hot air weave its way around me.
36, 36 degrees in the shade!

Francesca Maria Funnell (11)
Cotham School, Bristol

LIGHT

Light, it does not come at night, for it is bright!
Light, if you see it at night, it is not right!
For night is dark, and is not time for the park.

Light, it is bright. It comes from the sun,
Which can make you hot if you run!
The sun makes the day, and grows hay.

Light can burn your skin, but not your chin.
Light can make your car run, which helps you get things done!
If not for light, it would always be night!

Light makes fire, which can melt wire.
Fire can also melt ice, which is nice.
No one knows how, we have light now!

Lucas Down
Cotham School, Bristol

LIGHT

It wakes you up in the morning
And tells you when the day is dawning.
It shimmers on the lake beyond
The hills you look out upon.

Sometimes bright, sometimes slight,
It's the sparkle of a starry night.

Fighting through the autumn leaves
That are falling from the tallest trees.
It leaves a twinkle on the ground,
So shadows can lie all around.

Light is an essential, cast from above.
Light is life, light is love.

Ellie Clutterbuck
Cotham School, Bristol

LIGHT AND DARK

It was midnight and all the light and dark warriors
Were ready to battle!
3...2...1...Fight!
A hurricane and a tornado clashed and the battle began.
And as all hope seemed lost
A roar from Heaven and Hell echoed across the land
And in the middle of the army
Two dragons,
One from Heaven and one from Hell,
And the battle kicked up again.
The battle hasn't finished and never will.

Kez Briggs
Cotham School, Bristol

UNTITLED

She makes the world shine,
She brightens everyone's day.
Her joy reflects against the ocean
And everyone has a happy emotion.
The twinkle in her eyes
Is like the brightest star in the sky.
She is the light which we call the sun
And when she turns off, it's like the shot of a gun.
When you fall to the ground and close your eyes,
All you dream about is when it will die.

Kaya Campbell (12)
Cotham School, Bristol

ALWAYS THERE

Sunshine is a wonderful light,
It brightens our world by day
And comforts us with its rays.
Moonlight is just as magical
Calming, peaceful, asking us to dream
Its brightness lights our world.
A huge lantern in the sky
Always shining and never dies.
Starlight is a beautiful light
It brightens our world late at night.

Olivia Hall
Cotham School, Bristol

NIGHTLIGHT

Light, it is bright.
It shines through the night.
The glowing beam that flickers
And dances through the day.
It's the glistening reflection
Like a star on the window.
Every photon illuminates the scene
But every lustrous sparkle we all know
Is just like the sun.

Finn Ethan Webb (11)
Cotham School, Bristol

LIGHT

The bright beams of light sting my eyes.
As the twinkle of a star flickers in the night sky.
The misty glow of spark creeps into my room.
A fiery swarm of twinkling shine.
Shone in the distance like a star sparkling in the sky.
It is light.

Ben Luke Secker (12)
Cotham School, Bristol

UNTITLED

The glowing campfire shimmered in the evening breeze.
The blaze of light.
Light created by the glowing campfire
Could be seen from far away.
The heat of the roaring campfire was a lava.
It dripped on the palm of my hand.

Zach Mason
Cotham School, Bristol

BEDTIME

The light flickers in my room
As I think of all the terrible things that might happen to me.
Suddenly, the light goes out!
And darkness creeps into the colour
As I slowly close my eyes.

Rory Wilson Bopp (11)
Cotham School, Bristol

LIGHT

It sparkles in the day.
It twinkles when it's night.
It wears some sexy sunglasses
And gives off lots of light.

Maya Hay-Nicholls
Cotham School, Bristol

SEASONS

The green tree,
blows free
on a breezy day.

The brown tree,
has brown leaves,
that blow off on an autumn day.

The tree turns white
on a winter's night.

The tree with buds
Starts to break out.

Jessica Phillips
Cullompton Community College, Cullompton

MY POEM

Never say I love you
If you really don't care
Never talk about your feelings
If they aren't real
Never hold my hand
If you are just going to release
Never say you are going to
If you don't plan to start
Never look into my eyes
If you are just going to make me cry.
Never say 'Hi'
If you mean 'Bye'
If you really mean forever then try
But never say forever, if you don't mean it.
When you say forever
It makes me cry.

Anastasia Groom (12)
Cullompton Community College, Cullompton

SHARK ATTACK

I taste fear.
I see death.
Teeth as sharp as steel.
Coming closer and closer.
This is the end.
Goodbye life.
Goodbye air.
This is the end.
No tears be shed
For no pain I felt.
This is the end.

Ben Lewis (13)
Cullompton Community College, Cullompton

LOVER!

Her skin is as beautiful as the sea
She gives wings to you and me,
She is like an angel from Heaven,
Why has she gone away
When she can just come and stay?
Please come back into the warm arms
And never leave.
Always believe
And stay safe in your life.
Why . . . just *whyyyy*?

Caine Reece Patrick Jackson (12)
Cullompton Community College, Cullompton

THEY DON'T UNDERSTAND

Sometimes people around you won't understand your journey . . .
They don't need to, it's not for them.

They say that they do understand you but they don't,
They really don't know what it's like to be you . . . they never will.

They don't understand me . . . which is fine . . .
I guess it doesn't matter who I am.
They tell me to keep strong and keep fighting,
But they don't know that I have already lost . . .

Ella Louise Tucker
Cullompton Community College, Cullompton

FRIENDS

Friends are not the ones you chuck away,
they are the ones that stay.
You don't need to be there everyday,
But when friends need you, especially in May
Don't watch them cry!
Support them and try.

Chloe Phillips
Cullompton Community College, Cullompton

THE GIRL

Fat, stupid, ugly, some words that she's called
They kick her and slap her and her hair gets pulled.

They don't know what goes on at home,
As there, like at school, she is alone.

She sits in the corner of the room, lets loose all her tears,
Everyone around her, are her biggest fears.

Her dad's an alcoholic, her mum gambles all their money,
Then blames it all on her, it's really not funny.

When she's ill at home, she really isn't missed,
Her dad always reminds her that she wasn't supposed to exist.

She's resorted to cutting, her pain just gets released
No one really likes her, her ex best friend is deceased.

She's actually very pretty, and extremely smart,
And people would realise that, if they had a warmer heart.

She gets abused on Facebook, and other social sites,
But one day she decided she was not afraid of heights.

'Who jumped off the cliff yesterday?' asked the man who liked to slaughter.
The person turned around and said, 'Whom? That was your daughter!'

Aleisha Martin (13)
Exmouth Community College, Exmouth

IT'S NOT JUST A GAME

As the crowd cheers
And the players run out,
There's hisses and boos.
What's that all about?

This is a sport
It's not just a game,
Not about cameras
And the fame.

It's all about fun
And we all have a cheer.
At the end of the game
We all have a beer.

Running around
And kicking a ball.
The game could come down
To one single ref's call.

A tackle!
That's a foul!
What comes next
Is a row.

This is a sport
It's not just a game.
Everyone is there
Shouting your name.

At the end of the day
It's all a bit of fun.
Why should it matter
How fast you can run?

This is my sport
It's what I'm all about.
Play with no fear
And have no doubt.

Oliver Toomey (15)
Exmouth Community College, Exmouth

TICK TOCK

Tick-tock
away I go.
Shall I tell you what I've seen?
Would you believe me?

For I have seen shadows encompass suns,
I have seen smiles through glassy eyes,
I have seen laughter lines become tattoos,
I have seen new worlds created on paper,
I have seen the loss of a thousand in one
but do you believe me?

Tick-tock
away I go.
I am just a battery on the wall,
yet I still see light in your eyes,
when your heart slightly dies.

I have seen secrets shared with a saliva,
I have seen feet find their gravity,
I have seen doors slam in skulls,
I have seen hearts hold hands,
but do you believe me?

As I spin, you do not see these things,
life's simple happiness,
the universe's eternal sadness,
you just stare waiting for the thing.

Tick-tock,
believe me on this,
my battery will run out, as does yours
and when it is done I shall wish to take my eyes
and hand them to another to see the same things I saw,
could you say the same?

Kiara Mulholland (15)
Exmouth Community College, Exmouth

WHY DID THIS HAVE TO HAPPEN TO ME?

Waiting and waiting to hear the good news
Hearing the disease was gone from you.
Months and months nothing happened,
Why couldn't the doctors do something?

Seeing you lying there, just sleeping and not moving,
Made my heart feel like nothing
I remember the day when you lost your memory
And you didn't know anybody,
Not even me!

I thought you were getting better
But
Instead you were gone
You were gone from me and all the people,
Who loved and cared for you.

Why did this have to happen to you?

If you were here again
If only for one more day
I would listen to all you had to say.

But now it's too late,
You can't speak anymore
I wish I could change one thing,
I'd tell you that I love you!

No one will ever know how much you meant to me,
You weren't just my mum,
You were my best friend too.
And now you have gone, the world will never be the same.

Why did this have to happen to me?

Nat Lamphuengworn (15)
Exmouth Community College, Exmouth

WATCHED

I can't see them clearly but I still watch them
The takers.
As they change the most beautiful parts of the
Most beautiful planet
It was better when the stompers were there
Didn't change the land, just searched it
It was amusing to watch
All was well until the meteor hit Earth
I knew what was about to happen
New life, new terrain
I was excited
I hoped for smarter creatures
I got what I asked for
And more
They were building fires
Even though I am made of fire
It does make it harder to see them
Although what they were using it for was amazing
Houses
Clans
Villages
Towns
Castles
Cities
The new was exciting
But the more they made the more they took to burn and change
I can no longer see Earth
There is too much pollution
And how they travel over plants and ruin their natural beauty
I am ashamed to give them life while they destroy all I've come to
know.

William Pakes (13)
Exmouth Community College, Exmouth

THE FEW

Take to the air
Protect all that we know is fair
Dash up the ribbon of grey runway
Past the fields of golden hay
They search the cloudy sky
Knowing their fate could be to die
They see the enemy dashing forth
Coming from east, south and north
Their focused minds are full of fear
Knowing that conflict is very near.

A beastly Messerschmitt 109,
is in the Spitfire's firing line
Tommy opens up his machine guns
'Bombers on the horizon, there are tons!'
There is a Junkers on his tail
Bullets hit them like lashing hail
They're thinking of their treasured girlfriends
Hoping this bloody battle soon ends
Their comrades, pals are shot out of the sky
They're in this war but want to know why
They shoot some bombers, they plummet to the ground
They hope victory will soon be found

We lost many on that fateful day
What a terrible price it is to pay
But if you look closely at the reflection in the dew
You can still see our saviours, our heroes
The Few.

Alfie Blackham (13)
Exmouth Community College, Exmouth

THE AUTUMNAL SUN

'Tis late morning, cold and bitter. I lie here
on a park bench bathing in solitary company.
Around me are fallen leaves, each one a different
shade of yellow, orange, red or brown.
The autumnal sun glares down,
Beams beating on my face.

I stir and wonder, hidden by a cloak of solitude.
Now I know how he feels;
Different from you.
I walk the same paths I did yesterday, and the day before.
I know not why, but just do.

I watch the sky, 'tis not grey,
but almost every colour of an artist's palate array.
While the flowers die, black death grows behind the decaying shrubs.
As the autumnal sun sets,
Limbs of light thread through the trees and say goodnight.

Must be fun, to be the sun.
To play God to the mortal souls.
To have been there from the start of the first beating heart.
To have seen people deliver, destroy and die.
Should we pray to Him, does He care, would He even reply?

Back I go to my park bench and talk to the moon.
Nights are long and days end too soon.
So I lay down my head, think about life
And wait for the autumnal sun to bloom.

Ffinian Wills-Dixon (15)
Exmouth Community College, Exmouth

I AM THE SUN...

I am the sun as you can see
My power thrives through land and sea,
I watch lower life forms struggle to live
And you humans take for granted the life you live . . .

I am a burning star as you can see,
My strength is stronger between you and me
I helped begin the human race
And all you care about is the make-up on your face . . .

I am alone as you can see,
You look up in space and see me,
I'm stuck in this isolated place
And all you have is a smile on your face . . .

I'm heartbroken as you can see,
The coldness never bothers me,
But the coldness of your heart
Is tearing me apart . . .

I am the sun as you can see,
I provide heat so you're as warm as can be,
I produce light so you can see,
But you've never once thanked me!

Eleanor Jude Mills (11)
Exmouth Community College, Exmouth

THE RIVER AT NIGHT

When the golden light melts its last elegant dance, into the horizon
Silver glitter beams rest on the streams,
An eiderdown of tranquil for the night.
The glorious glisten keeps the water alive.
One elegant swan raises its admiring neck, absorbing its silent
surroundings.
Only a swaying reed brushing the relentless blue can be seen
breaking the serenity.
No human can hear the song of a distant grasshopper
As a family of water boatmen doze into a deep sleep under the
moon's superior gaze.
No animal is more powerful than silver orb who protects our sleep.
When we slip into a harmless rest,
Oblivious to a watchful silver glance from an inhuman being,
We don't notice the unbelievable force of the river life
Admiring the luck of its surroundings.
So before you rest, take a glimpse out that window
And turn your gaze;
For a moment you'll see it.
Right there.
Look!

Lucy Rose (11)
Exmouth Community College, Exmouth

I AM THE SUN

Stuck in an orbit of isolation
seclusion crippling my sanity.
My once constant state of euphoria
is now an intense state of despair.
I've seen the very first stages of
life and watched till the very end.
I've seen life thrive at my
expense, without a thought of gratitude.

I am seen as the magnificent; the greatest, but all without
appreciation.
I can throw oceans of ice,without
batting an eyelid.
With my knowledge, I can cause destruction.
But destruction is the cycle of passing.
My time is near, but not near enough.
To relieve my anguish and my sorrow
my final words have to mean something,
an experience worth accounting for.
Because the brightest ones fade the fastest.

Serena Dyke (13)
Exmouth Community College, Exmouth

LIFE

To you all,
I am the one who looks upon you,
I am the light,
I have seen death,
I have seen life,
I see you trust no one,
I see you help no one,
War is an aspect of your life.

I am the sun.

Harvey Tucker (13)
Exmouth Community College, Exmouth

A MAN'S BEST FRIEND

My life was happy and then it started,
My beloved dog and I were parted.
An evil cousin took him away
And I thought he was here to stay!
I used to walk him after school,
And now that's stopped, why is life so cruel?
He was my life, he was my joy
A soft burger was his favourite toy.
He used to dance, he used to sneeze
His favourite food was chicken and cheese.
He used to think that he owned the green
And the other dogs thought that was really mean.
We used to talk every day
And now those precious moments are taken away.
He was a beautiful boy, small, white and fluffy.
When he went to the dog groomer's, he came out all puffy.
I know why they call a dog a man's best friend
But Freeway will be in my heart until the end.

Amber Sturgeon (12)
Exmouth Community College, Exmouth

STARS

Sometimes the stars turn blue
Every time I am with you
But lying down would be in vain
You're always on my brain.
Take your time
I'll grab some wine
We'll stay up all night
I'll try to make things right.
We'll join the world beaters
Maybe even go to a theatre
We'll sit down watch TV
Maybe listen to your beats
If this doesn't make sense
I hope you won't take offence
I know you've been feeling down
But I remembered when I drowned
Sometimes I hear us singing
But do we get the same feelings?

Joshua Roswell (13)
Exmouth Community College, Exmouth

TEACHING YOUR CHILD A LESSON

Alone in a dark, cold and empty room,
Where did I go so wrong to deserve this heartbreaking suffering?
I almost feel like a half-twisted ghost,
Am I invisible to the people that make my heart throb?

Imagine their voices echoing against the half-painted walls,
The voice of kindly God,
The sudden rush of fortune shivering down my spine,
It will feel like pure gold!

I look around me on the hard, concrete floor,
Looking up at the cobwebs hanging from the ceiling,
The door was shattered into pieces just like me,
Feeling intense waiting for the moment I saw their faces.

I heard a familiar voice shouting for me,
Was it in my dream or was it reality?
Crossing my fingers in the hope it was them,
Mum, Dad you came back for me.

Yana Tushingham (15)
Exmouth Community College, Exmouth

A FRIEND

Eyes as blue as forget-me-nots,
Hair red as the sun,
I stared into her milky-white face,
And whispered, 'This girl's the one!'

We frolicked in the sea together,
We stumbled up a hill,
I got lost in her eyes somehow,
Just then time stood still.

Whenever I was lonely,
It was her I was beside,
Because I always needed her shoulder,
To be there when I cried.

So when people ask why I'm alone,
I tell them, 'Can't you see?
I don't need anyone else,
When my greatest friend is me.'

Daisy Schaechter (13)
Exmouth Community College, Exmouth

TIME

Rushing, wasting, mourning.
We live each day doing these things,
Finding this world far too boring,
Forgetting to listen whilst the birds sing.

We disregard what truly matters,
We disregard what's around us,
That is all until your world truly shatters,
The mayhem ends and so does the fuss.

You begin to cherish the moments that you didn't before,
You start capturing beauty that's only now noticeable,
Your mind accepts so much more,
The time you have, once felt impossible.

The clocks will tick but it is up to you what you do,
Go on an adventure!
What will you pursue?
Seize the day and find your treasure.

Alexia Tooby (15)
Exmouth Community College, Exmouth

BEING IN FOSTER CARE

At first I was distraught
And my self esteem went to nought
I was separated from my sisters and brothers
Why was my life different from all of the others?
I want to see my family more
Sometimes my life can be such a bore
I think about them day in, day out
It makes me so angry I just want to shout!
But now I can see, it's for my own good
Helping me develop into adulthood
Foster care really isn't that bad
At first I was upset but now I am glad
My second family are as good as my first
It honestly really isn't the worst
My advice to anyone going into care would be
Forget the bad things and just be happy!

Chantelle Fry (15)
Exmouth Community College, Exmouth

I AM THE SUN

The Earth was my best friend
But now he is just ugly.
It's them not me.
They treat me like I'm not here.
I see what they do
They make technology a reality
Rubbish, rubbish, rubbish
That's all they leave behind.
'Notice me!' I say
But they still pollute my wonderful world
They have wars in front of me
I see the pain
I see the death
I am so angry one day I will blow up
Who knows when . . .

Bradley James (14)
Exmouth Community College, Exmouth

THE PARASITE

The parasite is a creature of many shades; its true colours will never
be known.
It can turn green, red, pink and blue. It spreads its disease,
The invasive species.

It thrives by depriving others,
It takes its throne by burying its victims,
A consuming cloud of ash
Feeding off the earth
All at the expense of the benign being it depends on.
'Living in harmony with its environment'.

Drowning in their own chemicals
Trampled to death as they tried to flee the truth. The truth.
The coal cigarette that poisoned the world,
The nuclear chimney spewing the endless smog of death,
The radioactive waste they hide,
In a sarcophagus built in haste,
Their world would remain contaminated for the rest of their days.

It hides in its walls of cold concrete; it hides from the destruction it
causes,
It is the foulest being there is,
It consumes the most innocent of prey, the purest,
How dare it.

It dries the oasis,
It cuts down the leafy soldiers guarding the meadow,
It never satisfies its hunger.

Until it leaves a withering child, crying in the storm,
While it sits in its high tower
While it watches the poisoning of its world
Always looking to lay the blame elsewhere.

You.
The word for world is forest,
The word for human is parasite.

Natalie Widdecombe (15)
Hele's School, Plymouth

DEVIL'S DARKNESS

As deep darkness devours your soul,
The demon inside you consumes you whole,
Leaving your body like a blood shell,
Being dragged down to the depths of Hell.
His name's the Devil, the one you'll meet,
You'll be swallowed up by his ghastly heat,
In a pitch-black room you'll stay,
Until your body rots away.

You'll start to see things, the good, the bad,
And soon you will be going mad,
You're another pawn in his chess game,
And now things are going his way.
You're blind now, you cannot see,
You start to hear those deadly screams,
You can hear bones crunch and snap,
You're too afraid to even nap!

Now your hearing has almost gone,
You know that you were always wrong.
Around the room you now roam,
And realise that you were never alone.
Finally, you see what you could not find,
It was only really your crazy mind.

Ambehr Davy-Meredith (13)
Hele's School, Plymouth

HIM

Normality. It knocked,
I can feel the iron burning clothes,
Burning, burning.

I peeked and saw him,

His name had been everywhere!
The uniform of green and brown with a rifle
in his hands;
He knocked again.

I slowly made my way to the door,
Palms all sweaty;
Not sure from the iron or nerves.

I opened the door
Our faces brightened up.

My love was home,
Safe . . .
For now.

Rebecca Skelton (16)
Hele's School, Plymouth

THE SKY

When most look up at the sky,
They see the majesty of space,
It inspired man to fly,
And feel wisdom's warm embrace.

But what it shows for me,
Is our world's incredible grace,
For it inspires me to see,
And it puts me in my place.

The blue light shining past my eye,
Can be found nowhere other,
For humanity needs a family to survive,
And the sky is surely the mother.

So don't let the sky take you to space,
That's not what it is for,
The sky in all its glorious grace,
Shows us we need Earth so much more.

Joe Hannon (13)
Hele's School, Plymouth

THE DARK

(Lipogram – B)

The dark is lonely,
The dark is loud,
Full of untold fear,
And the unknown,
Clouds your judgement.

There's something out there,
Hiding in the shadows,
Just staring at you
Out the corner of your eyes you might even see it one day
It just floats away,
With a flick of a switch like it was never there.

Jacca Moran (11)
Holsworthy Community College, Holsworthy

WAY UP HIGH

Way up high
Where the birds fly,
Where dreams float round,
Without a sound.

Our every move,
Is being watched,
By a purple sheep,
Wearing a silk smock.

Ah, I bet you weren't expecting that,
What a wonderful, delightful change of plan.

Way up high,
Where the birds fly,
Where dreams float round,
Without a sound.

Our every word
Is being heard
By a green giraffe,
called Mr Mcsmurf,

Ah, I bet you weren't expecting that,
What a wonderful, delightful change of plan.

Our life is different,
Our life is weird,
Don't judge us,
Because revenge will be feared!

Tallulah Thompson (11)
Holsworthy Community College, Holsworthy

SEASONS

Spring, Spring, Spring,
Springing up and down in spring,
Springing with my toy spring in spring,
Springing with my spring lamb in spring.

Summer is the joy,
Of you and I,
Blossoming blossoms,
Blooming orchids all around,
My favourite season of all.

Autumn is amazing,
The time for Halloween,
Ready for a fright,
Boo!
Look at that face!

Snow is falling,
In the snow season,
Santa's on his way,
So ...
Hey, hey, hey.

Kaya Kirby (11)
Holsworthy Community College, Holsworthy

HALLOWEEN

Halloween, Halloween,
Spooky screams and scares,
The ghosts get ready, the houses and the creaking stairs.

Halloween, Halloween,
Spooky screams and scares,
Vampires arise from their coffins and almost trip down the stairs.

Halloween, Halloween,
Spooky screams and scares,
Pumpkins come alive and turn into goo!

Kayleigh Christine Rennie (11)
Holsworthy Community College, Holsworthy

MORTALITY

Day and night I think about what is approaching
To start failing my body down.

Tomorrow is a day that I will not abandon from my mind.

Continuous visits to that room await -
Most humans stand afraid at this point.

It's showing all signs that I'm not an odd individual -
Many humans gain it sadly.

I say out loud, 'Why is my mind blank?'
At that point it all floods back.

You may think it's just old folk, though it's not
It is young folk too – it's worst in young folk.

As I sit on a chair I look at my watch and spot that days and hours will pass
Just as fast as a sparrow hawk flying through a patch of sky.

My amount of days of which won't stay has passed by now. I think I should go now -
Look you got your way again, you don't go away do you?

Zoe Leigh (12)
Holsworthy Community College, Holsworthy

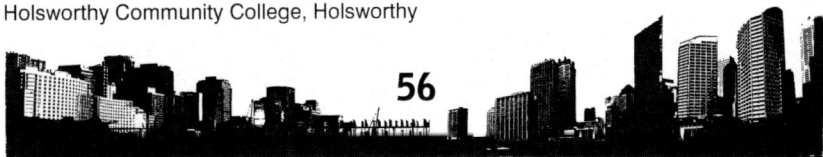

HOUNDS

(Lipogram – G)

Hot smelly hounds that bounce around the yard,
They shake and shake non-stop,
Slobber flies in every direction,
Up, down and all around,
Small ones, big ones, fat ones,
And don't leave out the skinny ones,
At the end of the day they are cuddly pets,
or hayfever pests!

Olivia Louise McMillan (11)
Holsworthy Community College, Holsworthy

BEAUTIFUL MARSHMALLOWS

These light fluffy,
Lumps of joy,
Have had little kids smiling,
For years,
Over beautiful marshmallows!

They have a kind of power,
The kind that keeps you eating,
Little pink and white sweets from Heaven,
My beautiful marshmallows!

The chubby bunny challenge,
Has made them more and more famous,
It's had us dribbling and drooling,
Over beautiful marshmallows!

You can squish them you can squash them,
Their taste is so divine,
That's the sound that people make when they see a fresh packet,
Gets the whole world smiling,
My beautiful marshmallows!

Alexandra Moore (11)
Holsworthy Community College, Holsworthy

LUSH SHOP

(Lipogram – T)

Gazing in my desired candy shop.
Rows and rows of shiny glass jars.
Luring me in, sparkling and shimmering.
Ding, ding, ding . . .
As I walk inside.

I feel overjoyed by aromas of delicious candy.
Masses of candy all kinds of shapes and sizes.
Feeling fuzzy inside.
Lush shop is my paradise.

Harry Grigg (11)
Holsworthy Community College, Holsworthy

MY ELLIE

I found my Ellie
In the safari
Drinking from the water hole.

When I was there
Guns were placed,
I shouted, 'Stop!' at the top of my voice,
Goodbye Mr Poacher!

Her trunk, tusks and tree stampers too,
They were all saved,
Saved by me.

I took care of her, the others as well
And today if you visit,
You will see pink teeth
All thanks to me!

My Ellie, my Ellie, all the others too,
My Ellie, my Ellie
How I love you.

Charley Hockridge (11)
Holsworthy Community College, Holsworthy

LUNA

(Lipogram – E)

Jumping high!
Hair as soft as silk,
Socks as bright as milk,
With a joyful mind,
Prancing tall as night's moon,
Bright brain,
Flaming tail,
But now within a grassy tomb,
Lying down in a dark void,
Staying still upon a grassy hill.

Rosie Sibley (11)
Holsworthy Community College, Holsworthy

ME AND MY PLACE

(Lipogram – O)

Waking up each day
I like this place in every way
Trees swaying, birds tweeting
While animals and us are sleeping.

The beauty in this place makes me smile
And I haven't felt sad in a while
It really is a treat walking my puppy
In such pretty fields, I am very lucky.

The hedges bursting full with berries
The grass green and bright
The clear blue sky up high
Making such a beautiful sight.

Being here is great
I really like it.
This is where I live.

Lauren Ruth James (11)
Holsworthy Community College, Holsworthy

LILAC

(Lipogram – E)

Lilac is a tingly thrill thing,
It kidnaps your soul away,
Startling flavour of plum burst,
At any bit of many days
It moulds you happy during your good months,
Upon your sad ways,
Don't worry lilac's always with you,
If you want a hand,
Don't wait to ask,
Lilac holds your soul,
It's always with you in your land.

Caitlin Johns (11)
Holsworthy Community College, Holsworthy

RAINCOATS ON HAMSTERS

Yellow raincoats on hamsters keeping them warm,
Dancing around the autumn-coated dorm,
Jumping in the pile of autumn leaves,
Sweeps up the hamster in a gentle breeze.

The freezing winter feeling closes in,
Watching their owners in blankets drinking gin,
The hamster is waiting for Christmas Day to come,
All the brand new treats and toys are so much fun.

The cold air begins to fade,
Spring flowers are being made,
The sun is now showing its face,
The hamster loses the scarves and dance with grace.

Hamsters sunbathe on the warm ground,
The summer feeling is all around,
Black sunglasses coating its head,
The light lasts longer which means longer before bed.

Georgia Stevens (12)
Holsworthy Community College, Holsworthy

POEMS

Why do we write them,
Why do we care,
I don't know, I really don't care.

Why do we like them so much, I don't know,
We find it a way to express ourselves, like I am now writing this to you.
I need to know the answer,
Of why we write them in acrostics or rhyme them.

So what is it that people find so fascinating about poems?
I guess we like to hear rhymes, just one moment,
We like it, they like it, everyone likes it.

Isaac Renshaw (12)
Holsworthy Community College, Holsworthy

MELONS!

You're juicy and round
You're spiky and green
You live on the ground
The biggest you've ever seen.

You start in spring
And end in summer
You get picked sometimes
What a bummer!

You get taken home
And left on the side
A knife is coming
You don't feel fine.

Oh no, it's above me
What should I do?
I will roll away
And then sue you!

Eve Langman (11)
Holsworthy Community College, Holsworthy

RED

Red. Blood. It means danger,
Sunburn and love,
Heaven and Hell,
They all fit into one,
They all connect together.

Red is annoying,
You have to stop for a red light,
You can't go there,
There is a red danger sign,
Danger sign, danger sign.

I like red and I hate red!

Natasha Ludwell (11)
Holsworthy Community College, Holsworthy

FLAMES OF FIRE

Flames burn,
They flicker like souls,
Flames explode,
As you read from the ancient scrolls.

Burning to a crisp,
You light up the sky,
As the yellow flames remind us,
Some day we'll die.

Burning and waving like blood-covered knives,
Rats surround as the floor turns red,
But for now we live our lives,
So it's all a mystery until we're dead.

All of this sounds sad but it reminds me of a wedding vow,
You may have heard, 'till death do us part,'
You might not have been touched by this, but you might be after this,
We will always be kept in memories in our loved ones' hearts.

Aaron Johnson (11)
Holsworthy Community College, Holsworthy

CAKE

(Lipogram – U)

Cake, a food made from layers of sponge
Forged together with icing.
Cakes are also covered in icing
Can have nice patterns and icing models.
Cakes are often made for birthday parties and other special occasions.
Cakes can sometimes have themes on that the person likes.
What is the world with no cake?
Cake is life!

Josh Drake (11)
Holsworthy Community College, Holsworthy

SPOOKED

Halloween, ah yes, the spooky time of year.
The time where people catch a horrible cold of fear.
The spooky pumpkin fellow,
That always seems to dwell-o.
Trick or treat,
You may get a tasty sweet.
Skeletons rising, zombies too.
Everyone hates them, oh but do you?
There are eight over there,
They just stink of dog hair.
Carving Jack-o'-lanterns, so much fun,
Come on, come on,
Let's spook Mum.
Sshh, it's the zombies, hide down by me,
I'm so hungry, give me some tea.
The zombies, eating a dead man, are hooked,
Don't touch that, don't, no, he looked!

Harry Sullivan (11)
Holsworthy Community College, Holsworthy

BEST FRIEND

I got your back,
You got mine,
You'll be there,
All the time,
To see you hurt and cry,
Makes me wanna weep and die
If we agree to not fight,
We won't care,
Who's wrong or right,
Hand in hand,
Love we send,
We will be friends,
Until the end.

Sophie Daniel (11)
Holsworthy Community College, Holsworthy

RAINBOWS

Rainbows make people stop and think,
Make people look away from their desks and kitchen sinks,
People will stop and stare, mesmerised,
Watch this awesome thing as it reflects in their eyes,
Some people say at the end a pot of gold
Will behold.
No one yet has reached the end,
If they do their damage will mend,
Leprechauns, the Irish say,
Will stay at the bottom to rest and play,
Never will anyone know,
If the myth will go,
However with lots of joy,
Great sorrow will come,
To get a great thing as so,
The rain will lash,
And bring the spirits low.

Becky Palmer (11)
Holsworthy Community College, Holsworthy

A DRINK FOR LIVING

(Lipogram – E)

It is a thousand things in a word,
Drips and drops of virgin soul and gold,
Shining your mirror portrait back at you.
Glossy, silky rapids twisting and twirling through paths to a salty drink,
It holds us conscious, it holds us tight.
Drinks of activity, drinks of growth, drinks of tranquillity.
Vastly variant in all it has to accomplish,
Filling its canvas fully, adapting to all situations.

Jaime Ley (11)
Holsworthy Community College, Holsworthy

WILD LIFE

(Lipogram – B)

At the crack of dawn the sun is rising,
It's a lovely day,
The farmers are up early preparing their hay,
There's singing coming from the trees,
And what a lovely melody,
As the day goes on, the wildlife stir,
A red fox appears with its shiny fur,
He's looking very mischievous . . . that's for sure!
As the sun goes down,
It starts to go dark,
The temperature starts to drop and cool,
All creatures great and small,
Are ready to settle down for the night,
Thank God,
He made them all.

Bradley Vile (11)
Holsworthy Community College, Holsworthy

AUTUMN

(Lipogram – P)

Short days and long nights, autumn is here
Fires are lit, winter is near
Children hunting conkers
Squirrels going bonkers
Chilly nights
Halloween frights
Red, orange and brown
I watch the leaves as they fall to the ground
Fireworks whizzing through the air
Everyone's snuggled in their knitwear
Autumn is my favourite time of year
Christmas is just around the corner, I'm full of cheer.

Abigail Dymond (11)
Holsworthy Community College, Holsworthy

THE DARK

The dark follows you,
It stays by your side,
It won't leave you until you die.

They come as shadows,
You can buy them online,
If you take it on a walk
Don't leave it behind.

Don't try to fight it,
You'll fall flat on your face,
You love your shadow,
Don't be a disgrace.

After all you can send it back,
if it won't go, give it a smack!
Wait, don't do that, you'll be in pain,
And then you'll never buy a shadow again.

Sophie Jennifer Hudson (11)
Holsworthy Community College, Holsworthy

DOLPHINS

Dolphins are so smooth,
I so want to swim with them,
Every single day.

They eat loads of fish,
Chasing after lots of shoals,
Under the caverns.

People on a boat,
Watching dolphins from afar,
Taking good pictures.

They're intelligent,
Dolphins save humans from sharks,
Every single day.

Symi-Amber Guy (11)
Holsworthy Community College, Holsworthy

THE SEA

The waves gushed against my feet.
I went to the beach every week.
The seagulls cried and the white horses galloped.
The sound of the sea rang in my ears.
This is the land of the sea.

The cliff towered up to the sky.
They dominated everything.
The pebble crumbled underfoot.
And in the distance was a small boat.
This is the land of the sea.

The clear blue sky hung above me.
No clouds at all in sight.
Rocks stuck up sharply.
And surfers flew across the waves.
And I am in it . . .

Ethan Ensor (11)
Holsworthy Community College, Holsworthy

THE UNIVERSE

(Lipogram – A)

The universe, big, empty, never ending.
Within, the void crimson sun rules,
Shining its intense red light onto some blue, green worlds.
Comets zoom through the sky,
Speeding to speeds of one million miles per hour.
The moon' s sphere, white, grey, sleeping in the sunlight,
Rising in the night.

Rohan Williams-Peck (11)
Holsworthy Community College, Holsworthy

THE ZEBRA

(Lipogram – U)

The zebra's kick to the lion is like
A lover saying no
The stripes are no cover
The only defence is
The chase
The chase is a game of
Tag gone to the extreme
'Help! Help!' the zebra calls
Yet friends evolve into
Traitors
For the risk is greater than
Forgetting the work that's from
Home.

Ethan Broad (11)
Holsworthy Community College, Holsworthy

DWARF RABBITS AND SNOWFLAKES

Fluffy little dwarf rabbits hopping in the snow,
Trying to win the best snow bunny show,
Snowflakes falling on their fluffy little tails,
Skating on a lake big enough for a whale.

Their long floppy ears dangling down,
All the bunnies are smiling, not one frown,
The bunnies put on their fluffy little socks,
They all stare with their big eyes up at the clocks.

One minute till Christmas, go go, go!
All the baby dwarf rabbits leap through the snow,
Can the baby bunnies fall asleep, no, no, no,
They stay up till Christmas morning and drink some carrot cocoa.

Evie Purl (11)
Holsworthy Community College, Holsworthy

A HOUSE

(Lipogram – U)

A box-shaped dwelling,
Which people live in.
It keeps family members warm and dry.
It has a strong frame to it,
Some are made from stone,
And others from timber.
They cost approximately £100,000 and above
Sometimes it stretches to £5 million!
They generally have several rooms,
Like a kitchen, dining room, living room, bedroom and bathroom.
It is a place where families gather together more often at teatime than any other time,
They vary in shapes and sizes.

Hannah Davey (11)
Holsworthy Community College, Holsworthy

OVER THE TOP

Going over the top is a horrible thing
The noise of the guns in our ears do ring
Climbing the ladder, going over the top
We are told to go forward, 'Don't stop, don't stop!'

Running through fields, friends falling down
The mud is so thick, nasty and brown
So close to the enemy, I can smell them now
Then that *bang* that sounds out, 'Oh God – ow!'

Connor Sweetland (11)
Holsworthy Community College, Holsworthy

SNOWY COLDNESS

Frozen fingers feel like arrow-headed glaciers,
A cover of ivory walking over fields,
Packing away swimming cozzies and unravelling our scarves and gloves,
Fog flying above frozen lakes,
Animals sleeping in comfy burrows,
Spring has come and now we can say, 'Goodbye snowy coldness.'
And say, 'Hello budding flowers!'

Elsie Whitaker (11)
Holsworthy Community College, Holsworthy

WINTER WONDERLAND

(Lipogram – F)

Winter has come, the temperature is dropping,
Nothing to do but watch the snow patterns gliding.
Alone, is something you make with yourself, yes a deal.
. . . A loved one dies, a seed will grow,
They will always have a winter wonderland inside of them you know . . .

Bella Jackson (11)
Holsworthy Community College, Holsworthy

FORCE OF ELEMENTS

(Lipogram – A)

The wind howls, the wind blows,
Over the roof it goes. Over the skies,
With the howling of wolves rushing through the sky,
Pushing the grey clouds out of the blue,
I will come with ferocity hitting your window,
Rustling the trees with power.

Chay Moran (11)
Holsworthy Community College, Holsworthy

AT THE PARK ONE DAY

(Lipogram – M)

I have a dog called Lou,
His favourite colour is blue,
He is seven years old,
He's like Harvey and never does what he is told,
We love it in the spring when we spend hours in the park,
We don't love the winter as it's always cold and dark.

Harvey Simpson (12)
Holsworthy Community College, Holsworthy

CHILLY DAYS

Wild wind blows
We will have snow
Brrr how cold
Especially when old
Will be nice
When all the ice disappears
And children have cold ears.

Shannon Louise Cockwill (11)
Holsworthy Community College, Holsworthy

BLACK

Black is the colour of darkness,
Black is the colour of the unknown,
It's the colour of your soul,
And your heart turned to stone,
It's the colour of your eyes frozen in fear,
Black is the colour of an ear-piercing scream,
Black is the colour of your killer!

Jessica May Wellington (11)
Holsworthy Community College, Holsworthy

TIGER POEM

Camouflage stripes to blend him into the grass,
Big strong legs to make him fast,
Whiskers to feel their way through the forest at night,
Long dagger canine teeth for killing its victims,
Long, sharp claws for grasping prey,
Paws so powerful they can knock their game over with a single blow,
So strong, a tiger can kill a buffalo, twice its own size!

Katie Grigg (11)
Holsworthy Community College, Holsworthy

BENEATH THE NOOKS AND CRANNIES

Beneath the nooks and crannies,
Ants scuttle,
Red as fire.

Beneath the nooks and crannies,
Spiders wind,
Hairy and small.

Beneath the nooks and crannies,
Leaves scatter,
A crunchy brown.

Beneath the nooks and crannies,
Old wrappers lie,
Sending off foul smells.

Beneath the nooks and crannies,
Little bugs are held,
Rainbow colours are spread.

Beneath the nooks and crannies,
If you look closely enough,
You will see everything.

Emily Wakeham (12)
Penrice Academy, St Austell

FAIRYTALE WORLD

Mallow-pink is the grass,
Blowing in the breeze,
Purple are the roses and red are the daisies,
Crimson are the high cliffs towering in the distance,
Yellow is the warm salty sea,
And dragons fly in the tangerine sky,
Red, green, yellow and purple,
Thump! Thump!
What is this sound breaking out in the peace?
A large white eagle,
Landing heavily on the flamingo-coloured ground,
Wildlife run in escalating terror,
For where there are eagles there are dragons,
Squirrels scatter like red paint flicked on a magenta canvas,
Grazing deer shower like drops of brown water,
As the dragon's scaly feet hit the ground,
A brave knight leaps on horseback,
The large chestnut rears and whinnies, scaring away the creatures of prey,
'Help! Help!' cries a melodic voice,
A nearby princess calls out in fright,
Threatened by an oversized sun-blue dragon,
All of a sudden she is tossed onto the horse,
Rescued by the gallant cavalier,
As she directs him to her palace,
The daunted dragon's never to return,
Deer graze quietly in peace,
Squirrels scamper around in neutrality,
White unicorns float softly down to Earth,
Reassured they are safe from the dragons,
And all live happily ever after.

Freya Morris (11)
Penrice Academy, St Austell

THE WILD WAY

Whistles and melodies,
Music in my ears.
The animals around me,
Without any fears.

As beasts they saunter,
Like fireworks they explode.
Raging, running,
Never exposed.

Not a destination,
Always an aim.
Surviving with threat,
Just like a game.

Whistles and melodies,
Music in my ears.
The animals around me,
Without any fears.

I can hardly detect them,
Adored and acknowledged,
As precious as gems.

Anonymous to the naked ear,
Loudly pounding thunder.
They scream, they cheer,
Banishing fear.

Survival is the mission,
No time to lose,
It's life or death -
You choose!

Jasmine Saunders-Berridge (11)
Penrice Academy, St Austell

FIRST IMPRESSIONS

(Inspired By Goodnight Mister Tom By Michelle Magorian)

Knock, knock on my door, gave me a surprise,
Opened to see the gazing eyes,
Children's faces like a dropless pool serene,
And there were women dressed in green.

'Morning Tom,' she said with a frown,
'I am the billeting officer from this town.
These are children from the city,
You take care of one, it's your duty.

For you I will assign only one.
Please take this boy, he's eight, quite young,
William Beech that is his name,
Quiet and shy, he's quite the same.

A home of religion his mother asked.
Close to a church, I saw as I passed,
Just look at the time, I really must go,
If there are problems just let me know.'

Off in a hurry
The children followed in a scurry.
'Come on Willie join me inside,
Don't be scared, there's no need to hide.

Just make yourself comfy.
This is my dog, Sammy,
You'll sleep in your very own room,
Let's go and eat, it will be dark soon.'

Jack Warren (11)
Penrice Academy, St Austell

KITCHEN CHAOS

Hiss, tick, ding, boom!
The steam is floating round the room.
Soup is splashing, chefs are dashing
To stop the cake from going *boom!*

The cooks are crying 'cause of onions,
Look out! There's a rat with smelly bunions!
Quick men, get out all your gun-ions,
Before it cannonballs in the soup.

Bangy, bangy, bangy! Boom!
Oh no, oh yes, it can't be true,
The rodent's not there, quick, search the room!
Before it steals the cheddar!

They hear a squeak and whip around,
Then look upon the plain, white ground,
The rat! It's trying to steal a pound,
Of delicious, squishy brie!

Down at the drain, the rat does run,
And out into the morning sun,
And he does have a lot of fun,
Eating his yummy food!

'Twas a glorious victory for the rat,
But also a fear and just like that,
He could have been nothing but a splat,
But he was happy he had the food!

Chanel Janet Wheeler (12)
Penrice Academy, St Austell

SCHOOL'S SUCCESS

I start a new school,
Where I don't get treated like a fool,
As I use a new tool,
That gets me through school.
This fantastic tool,
That I find cool,
Is only a word,
That I heard.
See your goal,
Understand the obstacles,
Create a positive picture,
Clear your self doubt,
Embrace the challenge,
Stay on track,
Show the world you can do it,
Because you're not stuck in a pit.
Success is a tool,
That I use in school,
I don't just dream for it,
I work hard for it.
It doesn't come to me,
I have to climb a tree,
To be able to succeed
I have to achieve!

Chelsea Pope (11)
Penrice Academy, St Austell

YEAR AFTER YEAR IN THE UK

Autumn leaves are falling,
The hatching chicks are calling.
The reservoirs are still,
No pollution that makes you ill.

The winter weather is coming,
Britain's wildlife is numbing.
From the sudden cold,
The animals have to behold.

Spring is here,
The animals cheer,
Britain is brought back to life.
Here comes the sun,
It's time for fun,
Songs play from a fife.

Summer's here,
Men drink beer,
Everyone's great,
And plays with their mates,
But the year is over
From Glasgow to Dover.
It's time for a new one
Let's hope it's a good one!

Thomas Richard King (11)
Penrice Academy, St Austell

EVACUEES

Standing on the streets
All alone,
Hoping that someone will let them
In their home.
Starving, suffering, they wander the street
Wet is one word to describe their feet.

Aaliyah Cleaves (11)
Penrice Academy, St Austell

AWAY IN MEMORY LAND

I lean my head in my hands,
I'm far away in Memory Land.

I remember crying, now it makes me laugh,
I felt emotion, if only by half.

It's my dad, he's leaving me!
It makes me sad, yet it makes me see.

No one is there forever, not even family.
I'm still away in Memory Land, and it's the way I'll be . . .

The rain falls, the clouds are crying
Burning heads, my heart is dying

You broke my heart, left me in pain
We fell apart, we broke in vain.

If it was love, it would be forever
If it was love, we would be together

The rain falls, the clouds are crying
Burning heads, as my heart is dying . . .

Kathryn Taplin (13)
Penrice Academy, St Austell

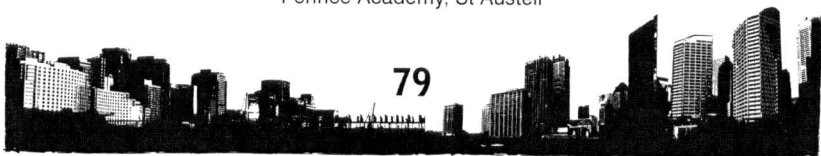

FREE SPIRIT

She gallops towards me
The grass slipping around her
Her mane flows free
Her tail streaming behind her
Her coat gleams
Her muscles ripple
The sun dances on her back
She shimmers in the light
She is stunning, breathtaking,
Majestic!

Emily Hoskin (11)
Penrice Academy, St Austell

EVACUATED

As skyscrapers start to disappear,
and grass begins to grow.
The air I breathe tastes far more clear,
and I see a blue stream flow.

The assistant comes with a folder,
as I fret about tomorrow.
I wish to cry on someone's shoulder,
while kids beg for their mothers in sorrow.

I watch the sun set,
and try to stay calm.
Yet I still fret,
will I live in a barn?

Fresh is the air I breathe in,
stars begin to shine.
I breathe deeply out and in,
once I'm asleep I'll be fine.

I hope.

Erin Rae Harris (11)
Penrice Academy, St Austell

THE WAY OF WAR

Bombs cascading through the sky;
Engulfing all signs of life,
Turning cities to ruins,
And hearts to stone.
The relentless war has come home!

The heat of crackling flames,
Chilled by the shrieks of death.
The hideous beauty of war,
Is not one you'll forget . . .

Maisie Craddock (12)
Penrice Academy, St Austell

LIGHT

A darkness saved by a fleeting glimpse,
Of light that spreads from within,
Getting weaker and weaker,
Until it reaches my toes.

A depth of shadows,
Lines the caves,
Until a flash of a torch,
Chases the darkness away.

The light gives hope,
It lights the way,
It takes away the nightmares,
Until sunset comes,

As soon as the light's gone,
The hope drains away,
As soon as the lights are gone,
They all lose their way.

Katherine Lee (13)
Penrice Academy, St Austell

A CLOSE SHAVE AT THE TRAIN STATION

The train is coming, it's slowing down,
But something's wrong. I can hear it now.
I look behind and suddenly see,
A train is coming. Whizzing at full speed!
The whistles are blowing, the sparks are flying,
The children in the station are whinging and crying.
This big scenery is breaking my heart,
When a woman jumps in the track, in front of the cart!
It's a big fat lady, as plump as a tart!
As quick as that, the train bounces off her belly,
And I heard a boy shout, 'Woo-hoo, go Aunt Nelly!'

Ashley Tinnion (11)
Penrice Academy, St Austell

MOUNTAIN BIKING

Wind through your face,
Hair running wild,
Rocks cascading downwards
Sweet forest air through your lungs,
Free as an eagle.

Jumping through the forest
With mud on your face
Sometimes in the night,
Sometimes in the day.

Streams trickling by,
Uphills make you pull
But downhills make you fly.
When you fall off,
You may even cry,
But you get up again,
With water in your eye.

Koben Carl Triggs (12)
Penrice Academy, St Austell

NATURE CALLING

Over mountains and under seas
Come the animals from here and there.
From the Arctic to the desert,
Here they come, here they are.
If penguin or kangaroo, they make their way here wherever they
come from.
Animals from north and south and east and west,
All come together now and here.

Sebastian Ludwig (12)
Penrice Academy, St Austell

WILLIAM BEECH

(Inspired By Goodnight Mister Tom By Michelle Magorian)

Bed-wetter
Story-adorer
Non-reader

Nature-novice
Misplaced-townie
Cow-discover
Stick-thin

Helping-hand
Badly-bruised
Continuously-cautious

Never-naughty
Perpetually-polite
Always-appreciative
Standing-straight!

Joseph Broughton (12)
Penrice Academy, St Austell

THE DANCE OF FRIENDSHIP

Friendship,
A new type of dance,
A unique beat,
A two-way street,
A catchy jive,
A moonwalk backwards,
Lasting until . . .

The music stops,
It's all over,
A buffering record,
A broken CD,
Until the next song
It's goodbye from me.

Katherine Ellen Watson (11)
Penrice Academy, St Austell

FRIENDS

Friends
Are like sweets
In a brightly lit shop window,
The sherbet: promising ups and downs;
A laugh, merry excitement
Bootlaces: long and peaceful;
Soft and sweet are always there.
Chocolate mice: warm, creating laughter;
But perhaps not made to last.
Although these all make us gleeful,
One problem still stands.
To separate the good from the best,
To locate a single sweet in the shadows;
Unique, bittersweet,
In no way perfect,
But perfect for me.

Abby Wherry (11)
Penrice Academy, St Austell

TOM AND WILLIE

(Inspired By Goodnight Mr Tom By Michelle Magorian)

Tom Oakley takes the boy in,
The notes says he's full of sin.
The boy named Willie is scared and sad,
For he doesn't know what's good or bad.

All things in the countryside,
Are the strangest things Willie could find.
With his new books and boots, he's happy,
His mom back home still cross and snappy.

Tom and Willie's relationship glows,
As Tom's kindness and compassion grows.
He stays happy until Willie is sent home,
After that, Tom's so alone.

Emily Passmore (11)
Penrice Academy, St Austell

OH WINTER, OH WINTER

Winds from the north whistle their flawless song;
Flakes of gems swirl soundlessly along;
Icicles hang unconsciously glistening;
Colours beneath the chilling sea began dancing.
Oh winter, oh winter, bring beauty beyond compare . . .

Cheeks flush with the colour of rose;
Fire of warming love effortlessly glows.
A tree of season spirits embellished with bliss;
Beams like the passion of a tender kiss.
Oh winter, oh winter, bring harmony beyond compare . . .

A creature scampers across the crunchy powder;
With its body tilted it began to ponder;
Its ears twitched and flickered like a candle.
Was the glacial breeze a challenge he could handle?
Oh winter, oh winter, bring curiosity beyond compare . . .

Stephanie Clemo (11)
Penrice Academy, St Austell

CUPCAKES

Cupcakes are sweet,
But could be healthy,
You make them look neat,
You don't have to be wealthy.

You decorate with sprinkles,
Whilst spreading on the icing,
The golden stars, on cases that twinkle,
Then let the juices flow with slicing.

They rise with flour,
It works with butter,
They're ready to be devoured,
They prepare you to mutter;
About your delicious delicacy.

Aliah Johns (12)
Penrice Academy, St Austell

85

THE FEELINGS OF WILLIE, AN EVACUEE

(Inspired By Goodnight Mister Tom By Michelle Magorian)

I'm scared! Where are we going?
Right now, there's no way of knowing.
My blood is pumping rapidly through my veins,
My life will never be the same!

Standing frightened, feeling alone,
Waiting for someone to give me a home.
Who will it be? Will they want me?
This is torture, can anyone see?

A stranger, his face wrinkled, his hair grey,
He grabs my bag and takes me away.
He looks mean and grumpy, does he have a wife?
And so it begins the start of my new life.

Michael Alexandar Ritter (11)
Penrice Academy, St Austell

LIGHTS

Eyes flickering with lust in the darkness
Sweat scraping temples of shifting bodies in smoke
Music slices through walls of billowing mist
They lose their sense of a tedious life gone stale
Lose themselves in the lights
Electric strands of pure gold
Carving into the souls of desperate mortal dancers blue, green,
orange, purple,
Hypnosis at its finest, it changes the dreary darkness of the club
Changes their souls with the lights
Walking outside back into reality
Closing eyes, sulking heart
I shiver in the summer darkness,
Fear scratching my shoulders
The moon comes out.

Cali Sage (12)
Penrice Academy, St Austell

THE WARNING LIGHT

The warning light flashed crimson
As it screeched for us to go!
A tsunami was coming!
There was not time to run,
No time to hide
Parents clutched their children
Not daring to let go!
Some ran to shelters
Desperate to survive!
The tsunami was coming,
Coming to drown
Hope was lost!
Fear was brought.
Brought by the
Tsunami!

Izzie Shryane (11)
Penrice Academy, St Austell

WAR

Bombs dropping everywhere, what will it hit and where?
Will it hit my house or next door?
I'm flooding with terror, shut all the doors.

I walk outside, what do I see?
I see screeching, walking, fire and of course, dead bodies.
My house is collapsing, I need to run.
Now where will I live? All is gone.
My rations are extinct, my house is dust.
My mum is gone, she is now at peace.
All I have now is my trusty bear, Rhys.
There is gas in the air, bombing all around.
No escape you will be found.

I hope we will be saved from this frightful war.
I hope it will end and it will be no more.

Emily Lord (11)
Penrice Academy, St Austell

RUNNING

I'm running from something,
That I shouldn't fear,
I don't know what it is,
I just can't look back,
What will it do to me?
I do not know,
What will it say to me?
I do not know,
Why can't I look back?
That remains a mystery.
I don't know what scares me more,
The thing itself or its appearance,
Just don't look back,
Keep moving forward . . .

Miguel Poole (12)
Redruth School, Redruth

LONE WOLF

The icy claws of night grasped the woods,
ripping, slashing and demolishing, squeezing the life out of it.
Like an anaconda constricting its prey.
The trees would groan and screech, as if in great pain,
Casting their mournful cries echoing off the bare tree trunks.
The shadows were prolonged,
stretching their bony fingers across the bare ground,
where tiny crystals formed making a shaggy rug of pure white.
These woods may seem like a frozen paradise, but if these woods you go
you will surely pay a price.

In shadows danger lurks,
Snapping jaws and razor claws.
Death from the sky or death from below,
it always ends the same, blood, blood, blood . . .
But some you see don't like that style,
they scurry and scamper, parading all the way.
They overwhelm their prey then silently tear it apart.

But these are small, but the one with the eerie call
can crush them all with one swipe of a massive paw
Its hungry eyes seeking, searching for a tasty treat.
It has fur like a smouldering fire
but deadly it is, hazardous, choking and deadly.
It stalks its quarry getting slowly closer, closer, closer . . .
Then it strikes.
Swift and precise sinking fang into flesh, claw into fur.
The victim soon stops struggling,
sinking down onto its knees in submission
taking its last breath in terror.
This time the killer will triumph leaving blood in its wake.
Yes, this is a wolf, lone wolf,
a shadowed beast
cloaked in mystery.

Skylar Kirby (13)
Redruth School, Redruth

ANIMAL ESCAPADES

At home I see, to my delight, my darling dog
Prancing along with her head held high,
Daisy is her name and what a sight,
Glossy black with silver specks. What a wonder!
I lean towards her and give her a kiss,
As I do I can hear her steady breathing,
She leans towards me and I can smell her doggy breath,
I can feel the delicate, smooth skim of her pink licking device.

At the beach I see a little crab hasten along,
And a dolphin twirling high above the sea,
The distinct smell of wet dog is hanging in my nose,
I can smell fantastic fish and chips wafting along the beach,
The taste of salt is hanging in the air,
When I lick my lips it is like licking salt,
I can feel the silky, golden sand sitting in-between my fingers,
The hard shell of the crab is making pain in my fingers
And the silkiness of the fish is cold and slippery.
I can hear the shrieking of the sea birds high above me,
The sea crashes down like a crane falling over,
The sea crashes down like thunder.

In the woods, the branches of the trees wave and whisper to the animals.
It is a cave of trees enticing me to travel forward.
I can smell the denseness of the wood's floor,
The distinct smell of pine and the fresh aroma of animal droppings,
As I race forward the delicate leaves skim my arms,
I can hear the cackling of carrion crows
And I can see the mischief-making mice making off madly.

Amelia Ellen Thomas (12)
Redruth School, Redruth

WRITER'S BLOCK

I can't think what to write.

That's it. That's the poem. Writer's Block.
Pretty self explanatory if I say so myself!
There's all these magical poems describing winter scenes
And dazzling landscapes, majestic animals
And then there's me
Simply me.
Someone has built a wall, circling my brain,
A prison for ideas, a straight jacket for creativity.
It's not like I'm avoiding being a cliche . . . well I am.
There's nothing wrong with those kind of poems.
The feathery white snow dances down to the icy lake . . .
Nah!
A fiery flame, hanging in the sky by an invisible thread,
Beating down on me as I stroll along the rocky . . . the rocky . . .

Ah! I can't do it!
I want to write things,
I honestly do.
All I want is to write!
If only there wasn't a rope tied to my brain,
Holding me back.

And so, I'm sat here, in the locked room deep inside my mind.
The room where only I have the key
And only I can set myself free
All I have to do is . . .

Try.

Jago Mottart (12)
Redruth School, Redruth

WINTER

Winter in the country is beautiful,
The lands are white with snow.

I see ice and snow,
The bitter breeze is cold.
The churches are bare and old,
I can see trees and a burst of sunlight.

Winter in the city is different,
The giant trees are covered in decorations.

I hear the roar of wind,
It's like a tiger's angry scream.
You hear the people singing along,
In a happy tune of song.

The trees are as bare as an empty page,
Covered in snow with sparkly crystals.

There's a lake outside my house,
It's as frozen as Jack Frost's heart.
Everyone goes skating,
In the cold breeze of winter.

Aimee Rebecca Kent (12)
Redruth School, Redruth

CORNWALL

The feel of sand under my feet.
Crashing waves demand defeat.
Skilful surfers ride foamy waters.
They look to the shore to see sons and daughters.
Fishing is like a great delight.
When you see a shark you get a fright!
The reef is a sharp dagger.
If you're not careful you will get a snagger.
My love for Cornwall only goes on...
I get very sad when I am gone.

Sophie Lauren Clifton-Griffith (12)
Redruth School, Redruth

POEM ABOUT DANCE

Not just moving whilst listening to the music.
Letting the music move you
Going where it takes you is the best
Taking each step with care is the hard bit
Easy as pie is the rest.

At first it's quite hard trying to get it right.
But once you stop listening
And start moving, you never want to leave the world that you have
just caught sight.
Yet no matter what you do you feel like you're winning.

You start to become the dance
And write your own story
But still it's all about taking a chance.

As the song starts to slow down and finish
You start to dance more calmly and copy the music.

Suddenly, you come to a stop, the song has finished
You stand there in silence, just how it was before.

Rosie Frost (12)
Redruth School, Redruth

AUTUMN

Autumn is a season
When the trees begin to lose their leaves.
The leaves swirl down towards the ground
In pretty colours such as red or brown.

They land on the ground in a tremendous heap
Children come and laugh and shout as they stomp through the piles
With leaves crunching under their tiny toes.

Autumn is also a time to spot conkers
And have a conker fight
Whoever is the strongest shall win.

Emily Barrett (12)
Redruth School, Redruth

SUMMER

The vibrant sky is filled with light
It is an amazing sight
That everybody knows is here, spreading cheer
Making a smile from ear to ear.

A sweet aroma fills the air even though nothing is there
It smells like fresh baked goods, sitting there attracting looks
In the window is where they lay
Just relaxing, chilled all day.

The sight of flowers growing in the light
Right by the deep blue sky
In a bed is where they lay
Sitting there every day.

The sound of kids having fun
Playing with their silly games
They all exclaim 'this is lame!'
As they blame each other for suggesting such a stupid game.

Jordan Jay Pearce (12)
Redruth School, Redruth

SHOW AND CIVILITY

It flies similarly to the way a pony trots with skill
And it must look stylish.
A ladybird a mocking bird any sort of bird
All birds fly as bright rays of sun.

It lands on my arms with a shrill hoot
Its dark brown wings fly across my body
In wind as thick as snow.
Our pupils look similar, dark colours of brown and black,
Its quill is dazzling again it is as dark as a shirt
But as dramatic as a thousand suns colliding into two.
I talk only of an owl, a dazzling owl,
A swooping, hooting, flying owl with striking show and civility.

Alex Fusco (12)
Redruth School, Redruth

FOOTBALL

Everything began with the shrill whistle from the referee
The overflowing bowl of people were chiding
The sphere morphed into me
I spun the orb into the cyclone.

Unexpectedly the towering hunk of brute like the seething bull
Knocked me down onto the jungle of lush canopies
He stole the sphere from my feet
But not for long ...

I sprung up, sprinting in the direction of the brute
He was in my sights
I slid into the hunk, while he fell and demolished me.

My legs picked me up, my nose began gushing with blood
No one's getting me now
The sphere rolled smoothly across the jungle
I didn't have control, I just pulled my leg back and swung ...

Ethen Gaylard (12)
Redruth School, Redruth

CHRISTMAS TIME!

The Christmas turkey sits on the wide metal plate,
Like a bird warming up her egg
The Brussels sprouts that lie on the china plate
Are bright green trees on the muddy earth.

The baubles covering the Christmas tree
Is the dazzling silver tin in the kitchen drawer
The bristles that had fallen off the tree
Are the leaves falling off the tree in mid-autumn.

The wrapping covering the present
Is a shining sun warming up the land around it.
The young child being given the present
Looks like a bundle of joy curled up on a dipping sofa.

Turaya Evans (12)
Redruth School, Redruth

AFTER ALL IT IS NUTELLA

As I go away I sense it there
With a happy aura, I dare to bear
Like a guilt trip, so worthwhile
A heap of bliss, a massive pile
Looking like a pot of pure gold
Always appetising, flavoursome and never old.
Smooth, sumptuous, silk feelings dribble down my throat.
On a tasty potential river in a boat
It tastes like love and sheer happiness
That takes away the sadness
Empty, empty jar
Like a pencil you never go that far
It is a silent voice screaming
Always smiling and always gleaming
It shields me, it is my umbrella
After all it is Nutella!

Esther Rodgers (12)
Redruth School, Redruth

A VERY SIMPLE THING

It's a very simple thing,
It flashes past the sky with its jet black legs,
It lands by my fingers and pretends it's a ring,
It stares right at the washing line, and lands right by the pegs,
It flutters by the greenery and crawls beside my bed,
It races at the end and races by the end,
It buzzes in circles right beside my head,
It's red, black and sly,
It's shiny, bright and shy,
But is it nice? Well that will depend.
It whizzes by the shelter as rain begins its falling,
It scales the walls and searches
But it's nature is simply quite appalling,
But beside the tree it always perches.

Nico Fusco (12)
Redruth School, Redruth

CHEERLEADING

Cheerleading, entertaining, energetic and enjoyable.
It is fast, dynamic and rapid!
Many people of all ages say that it's like a rapid wave.
Love it, or despise it?
Practises, drills, that's only the start!
I vow that it's tireless and hard work
Except it's enjoyable and a good time as well!
As energetic as a new born kitten.
The feelings that are inside!
Excitement, Happy!
The list goes on and on!
Weekly sessions, for all ages!
Academies, coaches, cheerleaders!
It's as lively as a crowd of crickets,
Do I want to have the time of my life?
Cheerleading is the answer.

Rachel Rapsey (12)
Redruth School, Redruth

SNOW

Snow in the mountain is fun,
But when the sun is here all the fun is done.

I see the flaky frost swirling speedily,
Towards my cold and numb face,
As the trees lose their leaves like my lace.

The gradual green trees are brightening like the sun,
So it covers all the fun.

The wet squelchy snow crawls up my leg like a nest of ants.
So now here's the sun,
I say goodbye to the fun,
While the snow goes out.

Piran Phillips (12)
Redruth School, Redruth

GOAL

Tackle, save, corner,
Cross, header, goal!

Pass, talented, midfielder,
Through on goal!

Taken, pace, counter,
Near to a goal!

Tackle, penalty, horror,
Lining up the goal!

Suspense, drama, goalkeeper,
Tremendous goal!

Matthew Watters (12)
Redruth School, Redruth

THE BEACH

The eroded rock crumbles between my feet
While I amble along the remote beach.
The glimmering water, icy cold
Break into the rock
Like they're acting all bold
Ice cream drip onto my feet
But I don't care, it's a nice treat
I love the beach, it may generate smiles
Even though the weather will be wild.

Olivia Iles (12)
Redruth School, Redruth

THE FOREST

It is a labyrinth of twisting, elegant trees,
It is an ocean of colourful, silky leaves,
It is a place of relaxation and peace,
It is a public house of happiness and ease,
It is a cage of deep passion,
It is a showcase of natural fashion,
The forest is a city of wonder.

Ella Davidge Brown (12)
Redruth School, Redruth

DEPRESSION

I'm frightened I'll fall,
I'm terrified I'll get hurt,
I'm afraid you'll go,
Without another word,
You won't even tell me why,
The only word you'll leave me with is
'Goodbye.'
I'm anxious about all these,
Words in my head,
They send me to darkness,
Depression is a war,
Just with yourself,
Every thought is a bullet,
Every wound is triggered by you,
Every movement kills me,
Your lie's the bullet,
And your mouth's the gun,
I've got blood on my hands,
And stories I will never tell,
I wonder why you can hurt me,
But I can't hurt myself,
After all,
Weren't we born to die?

Morgan Latham (13)
Ridgeway School, Plymouth

PLAYGROUND BULLIES

It's wrong you know
What you did to me
Maybe it was abuse
But it was done so subtly
Taunting me
With words and looks
My safe haven
Found in the pages of books
I escape this world
And enter theirs
Where anything could happen
And no one cares
The real world is harsh
People point and they whisper
They laugh in your face
And say, 'Look at her.'
It pains me now
To think back to those days
Of playground bullies
And so many tears of pain
It was okay for a while
To live that way
But school got worse
With each passing day
The kids grew up
But the comments got worse
'You're filth, you're scum
Your life has no worth.'
No one knew, no one saw
But I found my friends and the pain was no more.

Faith Heney (14)
Ridgeway School, Plymouth

DEATH GAME

Stage 1: kill an evil chicken, then another
I slaughter them all, including their mother
It doesn't matter, it's just a game
This is a virtual world where I have no name

Stage 2: the cow lords eat but I gun them down
They all die so I'll take the demon crown
This is already so fun
The river of blood is more beautiful than the sun

Stage 3: fight against the gorilla boss, eventually I stab his heart
I eat the thing whole, it tastes just like tart
Level up! I have more power
It will be useful in ascending the victory tower

Stage 4: I lob an incendiary grenade on the floor
The poisonous slugs shrivel more and more
Finally, I unlock the 5th stage
I rest to restore my stamina gauge

Stage 5: pitiful humans attack me when I'm unaware
They attack from all angles, it's unfair
I get shot in the leg then in the heart
Game over! Press 'X' to restart.

Jordan Combs (14)
Ridgeway School, Plymouth

TRUE LOVE

T rue love is a gift
R eceiving it is even better
U nder the stars they kiss
E veryone can have it, if only they try

L ove between two people who love
O ne another
V alued when it's there
E specially missed when it's not.

Lauren Hampson (13)
Ridgeway School, Plymouth

YOU WERE THERE

I came home, fired from work
Screaming that it wasn't fair
But I didn't have to worry
Because you were there.

I came home crying,
Saddened at my living nightmare
But I needn't worry
Because you were there.

I came home ecstatic,
Which was very rare
And what made it better
Was that you were there.

I came home traumatised,
I thought no one would care
But I was wrong,
Because you were there.

I came home broken,
My heart about to tear,
And became so much worse,
Because you weren't there.

Ethan Wilshaw (13)
Ridgeway School, Plymouth

FISHING

When you go fishing it's so cool.
It lets you think.
Sometimes you chill.
Sometimes you bring lunch.
You need to dress in good warm clothes.
When you fish, you may catch a Pike.
They're very strong, they pull you round.
They've got sharp teeth, so beware!

Oliver Buckman (13)
Ridgeway School, Plymouth

LONELY

(Lipogram – C)

She seems happy all the time,
She's always smiling,
She laughs,
She jokes about,
But deep down she's sad, lonely and broken,
No one knows this,
She keeps it to herself,
She doesn't want people to feel sorry for her,
Everyone she thaws to,
She's afraid of being forgotten,
They stay in her heart but not in her life,
The old happy her is gone,
And there's
only one reason for that,
The reason is . . . she misses someone,
Someone that used to treat her like a queen,
Someone who thought the world of her,
Someone who has now moved on,
And found someone else.

Jodie Newport (13)
Ridgeway School, Plymouth

CURIOSITY

Curiosity is turquoise
It is young and adventurous
It is a toddler walking their first few steps
It is a kitten exploring the outside world.

Curiosity tastes like when you try a new food
Refreshing, intriguing
It sounds like a sailing ship
It feels like an oversized coat
It looks like the ocean waiting to be explored.

Jack Kellett (13)
Ridgeway School, Plymouth

103

HEART BEFORE THE OARS

Attention is the word that strikes our senses,
Go is the word that lights the vicious stir,
Don't get too cocky, you might not be so lucky,
As this is the race which steals the breath from your lungs,
Tears the bare skin from your hands for blisters are this season,
Careful now, pace yourselves, speed ain't smart,
Quads galore, singles ashore,
Taking on the raging tide,
Strength is certainly not a thing to hide,
Your war cry is ten powers that is the water to your flowers,
This is no walk in the park my friend,
For this may come to a 'watery' end,
Hold steadfast, keep your balance,
Keep in time, no crabs to be had,
You're nearly there, the end's in sight,
It's time,
It's time,
Release the Kraken!

Phoebe Jayne Lansley (13)
Ridgeway School, Plymouth

GOALKEEPER

I'm the keeper, I save the ball
I'm the winner of them all
I never let the ball past
Because my hands are very fast
I deflect the ball with my feet
The fans are not scared of defeat
I play in strike
And I skill past the defender called Mike
I kick the ball at the net
Everyone place their bets
We always win our games
Because the other teams are lame.

Ben Jesty (13)
Ridgeway School, Plymouth

HAPPINESS

Happiness is yellow,
Sunny and bright,
Happiness is yellow,
The morning light.

Happiness is orange,
A joyful sun,
Happiness is orange,
Kids having fun.

Happiness is blue,
Crystal and clear,
Happiness is blue,
Never having fear.

Happiness is gold,
Shiny and new,
Happiness is gold,
Happiness is in you.

Rachel Wren (13)
Ridgeway School, Plymouth

DEEP DEPRESSION

Depression is the colour of grey.
It basically pushes you away.
Like a fog clouding emotions,
On a cold misty day.
A coat wrapping you in despair
Tasting like ashes falling through the air.
Like an enormous void,
Like you don't even care.
It feels like a giant weight replacing your heart
Like a game of tug of war pulling you apart.
Getting rid of bad habits,
But it is hard to quit once you start . . .

Jack Skidmore (13)
Ridgeway School, Plymouth

NYX

Lurking in the shadows
At the edge of vision
She is clothed, not in black
But in blackness

Ubiquitous fear;
When you hear her name
Shivers run down your spine
Her eternal embrace; cold and dark.

Goddess of night
Never to be seen
But always to be felt

Hiding in the black opaqueness
Waiting for that one opportunity
To silence her foe
To blacken the world.

Sam Stokes (13)
Ridgeway School, Plymouth

NETBALL

I worship this sport,
In anything that I think.
I adore winning,
Also grinning.
My team is like family,
They all make me happy.

Netball is fun,
I love to play in the heat,
I play wing defence,
It gets very intense.

I love netball,
Netball is my passion,
A lot more than fashion.

Cody Morgan Norris (14)
Ridgeway School, Plymouth

LOVE

Love is the colour of red crimson.
Love is what you feel for that one person.
Whenever we're apart I miss you!
Why are you so handsome?

Love is what you feel in your heart,
Like strings pulling you apart.
I cannot live without them!
It brings me a new start.

When you're not with me I don't feel whole.
Maybe even, sometimes cold.
You help me find my way,
You make me feel like precious gold.

My one true love is my phone!

Devon Moran (13)
Ridgeway School, Plymouth

SWIMMER'S MENTALITY

We wake up in the cold dark,
No one's at the park.
Everyone thinks we're crazy,
Especially my mate, Maisie.
We seek pain,
But we will always gain.
We find strength,
But we are only on the tenth length.
We jump in an ice-cold bath,
But much better than math.
Feeling sick after hard sets,
Me and my dad are always making bets.
I don't give a damn,
But that is who I am.

Elle Jade Carne (13)
Ridgeway School, Plymouth

INSIDE

Inside it's dark, empty, alone
A constant ache of sadness, a pit of emptiness
The thoughts that burn in your head
Ugly, stupid, no one wants you
The world is black, dark and lonely
The emotions like forces, cancel each other out
Your head a vast, misty and gloomy mess
Hatred seeps through your veins
The negative thoughts penetrating your every move
Loneliness turns into sadness, sadness turns into anger
Anger turns into violence
The sinking feeling when someone leaves you alone
Happens so much you can't even feel it
It's just always there.

Sarah Lyon (13)
Ridgeway School, Plymouth

GREY

Grey is a dark horse
The last one to be picked.
They say, it's dull. It's depression itself.
Cold, dark and lonely.
Like an obsidian abyss.
But sadly to some,
It is familiar,
It is right.
People get put out and become friends with it,
Because of illness or physical features.
Don't let this happen.
It must be alone.
Grey must be grey.
And grey must always be alone.

Harry Holgate (13)
Ridgeway School, Plymouth

POLAR EXPRESS

Polar bears, so cute and fluffy,

When they roll around, they soon turn scruffy

They can be very scary,

Just as scary, as they are hairy

More to come, so many flaws,

Such as the very sharp teeth and claws

They tend to eat a lot of meat

They catch prey to have a treat.

We all know they're such a delight

Pick on one, you'll start a fight.

Aaron Hodge (13)
Ridgeway School, Plymouth

FIRES OF FURY

Blazing and luminous,
Warm and cosy
Crackling and hissing
Red, oranges and yellows
Flushed face and hypnotic flame
An emblem of flames.

A row of elder flames
A seal of millennium flames
A sword of raging fire
A budding flame
Scorching marks
Flames of courage, hope, friendship and love
Fire will always leave a mark.

Sean Wallis (14)
Ridgeway School, Plymouth

LOST BUT NEVER FOUND

She cries at night in a pit of fear
Tell her 'get up my dear'
She picks up the knife
Thinking of her bad life
She's almost gone
Help her live on.

You have one more chance, right?
And it's tonight.
Help her before she goes
Make sure that she knows
You'd do anything for her
You love her man,
Why don't you just tell her?

Leah North (14)
Ridgeway School, Plymouth

RED

Red is anger,
The flames in eyes
A raging inferno.

Red is love,
Passion and affection
Heartache and despair.

Red is pain,
A river of blood
A scar on a face.

Red is danger,
A stop sign in a road
An escaping lion.

Jonathan Watson (13)
Ridgeway School, Plymouth

THE GORGEOUS BEACH

The beach. Gorgeous, stunning
Shimmering seas catch my eyes
Sand between my toes
The sea
You hear the roar
Of stones, where the waves draw back
Bare-footed by the water's edge
The burning hot sphere high in the sky
The soft dry sand behind the water's edge
Night descends
The moon's shadow on the water's edge
Waves dancing in the shadows
That was my time at the beach.

Alicia Christina Collihole (13)
Ridgeway School, Plymouth

SCARIEST DAY OF MY LIFE

This is the scariest day of my life,
I'm walking home with someone following me,
'Start to walk a little faster,' I say in my head,
That someone does as well,
I start to panic,
Start to jog,
They do it as well,
I start to run faster
I trip and they come to me,
I hide my face,
I wake up,
To find that this is a dream,
I guess this is what is called a nightmare . . .

James Brokenshire (14)
Ridgeway School, Plymouth

LOSS

Loss is a cobalt colour,
It is hopeless, bitter.
It is the colour of your tears
As you cry a river.
It is the end of the life,
The end of everything to you.

It tastes like lemons,
Sour, pungent.
It sounds like a thunderstorm in your mind,
It feels like charring fire inside your mind,
It looks like you no longer have a soul.

Jack Havard (13)
Ridgeway School, Plymouth

HORSE POEM

(Lipogram – I)

Strong and powerful,
The creature you can depend on,
The beast that mentally tests you, pushes you, advances you,
Over to the gates he elegantly trots,
Teddy's flaxen mane flows through the breeze,
Just me and Teddy versus the world,
The struggle of control when he won't stop,
He bolts, bucks and rears,
From the usual dupe fear,
But the trust and love last forever.

Kirsty Wroe (13)
Ridgeway School, Plymouth

TENNIS

T ennis is the life of sport,
E very ball has to go over the net,
N ever argue or shout,
N ever hit the ball out,
I s there going to be a let,
S omeone's got to win,

S ome silly mistakes,
T he balls are hard and light,
A re you up for the fight?
R un to the net, volley, smash and win your right.

Joe Puckering (13)
Ridgeway School, Plymouth

LOVE IS...

Love is pink.
It's like a bright blossoming flower.
It feels like butterflies fluttering in a meadow.
It's beautiful, it's sensational.
It feels like the most comfortable sofa
Always there to support you.
It sounds like a stunning bird
On a summer's morning.
It's like a security blanket
Which wraps you in your own world.

Lucy Chapman (14)
Ridgeway School, Plymouth

REVENGE

Revenge is blood red,
It is pure darkness, evil,
It is death at its finest,
It is the end of life.

Revenge is like a sharp knife entering your stomach,
Painful, hurtful,
It sounds like a massacre of innocent civilians,
It feels like your soul is being torn apart,
It looks like someone being burned at the stake.

Edward Thompson (13)
Ridgeway School, Plymouth

SPRING

Rabbits thump their feet
The sunshine reflects the emerald-green grass
And tulips are a magenta pink.
Bees buzz and sweet hummingbirds sing.
Spiders spin silver webs.
Purple metallic dragonflies shimmering in the sun's rays.
Water dances with tadpoles' ripple.
The lime green frogs bounce around like rubber balls
And fire their tongues like cannons.

Jonathan Rowse (13)
Ridgeway School, Plymouth

FAKE SMILES

Smiling is like a disease,
It's almost everywhere you look,
But it's not always real,
They might smile on the outside,
But on the inside they're dying,
They might be happy,
They might be sad,
But you don't know the life they've had.

Mathew Lake (13)
Ridgeway School, Plymouth

REJECTION

Rejection is white, bitter like a sour lemon.
It is feeling unwanted, uncared for and alone.
A stab in the back that's as painful as death.
A blank piece of paper that no one's signed and never wants to.
It is the flame of Hell, always being thrown at you.
Rejection stays with you until every bone in your body is burnt and
left to turn into ashes.

Rose Whiteley (13)
Ridgeway School, Plymouth

AUTUMN

A utumnal leaves fallen
U nder the golden trees
T ime and time again
U nder the trees with years of history
M oist from the early morning dew
N early a year gone, it's time to fall again.

Aimee Bullen (13)
Ridgeway School, Plymouth

ALONE

Suddenly I become aware,
Of the empty seats, there and there and there.
I put down my sandwich momentarily,
When a huge girl growls at me scarily.

Behind her, she has an army,
With Sarah Jones, a load of boys and of course, Lily Jarmey.
They glare at me, their eyes a constant gaze,
Why do they bully me in these ways?

They know about my loneliness very well,
They know about my shy, shy shell.
Then their faces break into a smile;
I have seen this coming for quite a while.

They tease, point, giggle away,
Which is the case every single day.
I sit by myself, eat lunch on my own,
Hoping my tears haven't yet shown.

The rumours are true, I have no friends,
So people tell me to go and make amends.
But I have never argued, fought or done wrong,
It has just been like this all year long.

I don't understand why I can't be liked.
Is it my face, my grades, my height, my bike?
I am left with no idea at all,
Why I am the most hated person in school.

There is nothing I can do if I don't figure it out.
But I am purely detested without a doubt.
For a long time, I have truly known,
That for the rest of my life, I'll be completely alone.

Kelsey Payne (12)
Royal Wootton Bassett Academy, Swindon

THE DAY I DIE FOR HIM

I can taste my metallic blood,
I'm excited but nervous,
Giving up everything for a brighter future for everyone,
I look out the window,
My last glimpse of daylight?

He will be proud of me,
I will have a better life there,
When I join him I know he'll be proud.

They're painting me up,
So I look good for him,
The guards have come for me
I can see my final sunrise just over the mountain,
We are walking to his teocalli,
It's a quick walk but it feels like we've been walking for an eternity,
Savouring every breath, swallow and step,
I see the top of the temple in the distance,
Before long I'm faced with the long climb.

My heart is racing so fast it feels like it's trying to break out of me,
Every step means twice as much as the last,
Every breath means twice as much as the last,
Every swallow means twice as much as the last.

The daunting climb is now laid in front of me,
I'm ready.
I look around, everyone's eyes fixed on me as I start to make the
climb,
I'm now ready to move to the next life,
He draws the knife,
I look up and pray to him, Huitzilopochtli . . .

George Moore
Royal Wootton Bassett Academy, Swindon

PRISON

Stuck, staring up, my eyes met his.
A tingle in my spine, a clasp in my throat.
I turned my head; his eyes still glued on mine.
Frozen. A look in his mouth that is similar,
But different to none. A gloat.
I knew why I was here. Him.

My fist clenched as a symphony of pain rushed through me,
The second hits were harder, right above my knee
Yet I repelled, I would not flinch.
I whacked but it was a pinch
Not tough enough or rough, cut off
He knew why I was here. Him.

He murderously gazed into my thoughtless brain
All my ideas but nothing dared come
As I looked down at his muscular legs
A cut redder than a frozen nose was ablaze
And all I could think was the pain that I'd caused.
He knew why he was there. Me.

I felt my neck gag, and my spine tingle
My mouth opened but no sound, yet a sprinkle
I burst into tears.
Should I have got in that dangerous knock down?
Was this man really guilty for the damage he had caused us.

We both knew why we were here,
We both knew how
But what we didn't know was how would we get out of
Prison?

Hope Mary Ashford
Royal Wootton Bassett Academy, Swindon

GLASS HEARTS

Our glass hearts,
Too precious to be untouched but too strong to even be crushed.
They give us our roller coaster like life,
But make one wrong move and it will be spilt with your invisible knife.

Our glass hearts,
With us from the start, to the very last beat,
Because then our clock stops and we will no longer rise to our feet.
It is the beginning to our story so a new page will begin,
And our book of life will have funny stories to tell within.

Our glass hearts,
Work extremely hard, every second of every day,
And it will slow down as we get grey.
Loved ones may whisper sweet nothings onto a new page of our book,
And that is when our core is hooked.

Our glass hearts:
Hold the life like a circus,
And some people may think they are worthless.
Most people use them as a target, trying to hit it in the middle,
Shouting and screaming with glory to give your heartstrings a twiddle.
Stay strong, hold onto those precious moments that your glass heart holds,
Because at the end of the day they are filled with your gold.

Bindiya Hadani (14)
Royal Wootton Bassett Academy, Swindon

NATURE'S PATH

Just as the oak grows from an acorn
A majestic tree from a humble beginning
High in spirit and life, you are freeborn
Who knows what the distant future will bring.

As you grow and develop in size and confidence
And as peace and love fill your heart
You bury your nose in the flowers' fragrance
And the young sapling admires its juvenile counterpart.

Once it sheds the mantel of childhood
The oak blossoms into its own mighty glory
You take your place in the world of adulthood
In love, you scratch your names in the trunk contentedly.

From mighty oaks tiny acorns ripen and fall
A new generation of saplings growing
Laughing, giggling and sprouting tall
From beneath the shade of the branches bowing.

A frail grandmother and the ageing oak
Sit blissfully watching the world go by
Reflecting on their developing family and kinsfolk
The stress of time weakening body and branch with a sigh.

As the winds blow, the majestic tree falls one last time
Calm descends like a dream-filled sleeper
As time and place fade away, the funeral bells chime
Both are gone, but fond memories linger.

Elena Canosa (12)
Royal Wootton Bassett Academy, Swindon

PENNY

Penny is my gorgeous pet,
The sweetest little pussy.
She likes to nibble on her food,
But often is quite fussy.

Such a frightened puss, she will produce
Lots of meowing noises
When frightened or excited,
Or when messing with her toys.

Her colour is like the night,
With white sploches on her feet.
So soft her fur, cuddly too,
She is so very sweet.

Little gorgeous pussy,
Wild, excitable pet.
Sleepy, dozy, very snuggly
She is the best you'll ever get.

Noisy, white, moth hunter,
Friendly little pussy.
Her biggest secret is,
She is the biggest wussy.

Katherine Channing
Royal Wootton Bassett Academy, Swindon

HAPPINESS WILL COME

Sharp, cold winds carry enormous loss
Blood-dyed grass of No-Man's-Land holds sadness.
However, I will never lose mine for fallen soldiers.
Happiness will come.
We will hold a silence regardless
We have no need for sadness.
Happiness will come.
Happiness is here.

Olivia Crowley (11)
Royal Wootton Bassett Academy, Swindon

THE ACCIDENT

He clutched his aching arm,
A pestering sound in his head rang like an alarm,
His leg was plastered into a strong cast,
The doctor said the recovery would not be fast.

She woke to a blinding bright light,
Her body was enveloped in an excruciating pain she could not fight,
Her eye was black and throbbed like a steady drum,
Her face was a blanket of blue bruises making her face feel numb.

He writhed in agony and pain,
He lashed at the doctors who knew he was insane,
Anger coursed through his veins,
He pictured the cruel man stalking away from the crash in the rain.

The prisoner clenched the cold, dull, iron bars,
He was the villainous man who crashed the cars,
He laughed sinisterly while remembering their lifeless faces,
Torn and ripped, bleeding onto their leather briefcases.

Friends and family watched the coffin lowered into the ground,
All that could be heard was a faint, morbid, sobbing sound,
He was dead, she was dead,
They were dead.

Jack Clarke (13)
Royal Wootton Bassett Academy, Swindon

FIREWORKS

Flickering fire swirls into sight,
with rockets exploding off into the night.
They rise like sudden fiery flowers,
then drop to the ground in shimmering showers.
Purples, reds, golds or blues,
crowding my eyes with their glorious hues.
Spinning wheels whistle whilst fireworks shoot high.
Crowds cheer loudly when the closing fireworks die.

Lauren McKenzie (11)
Royal Wootton Bassett Academy, Swindon

A WORLD TAKEN OVER BY TECHNOLOGY

Ringing and beeping phones on a table,
Friendship is in the air.
You can hear the pain of laughter as they giggle frantically.
Books and reading are now long gone,
And dreams are turned into nightmares.
Now, the new generation is full of technology,
And the old ways are left behind.

A world of modern equipment,
Different and confusing.
Now everyone is caught up in their own world,
Of texting and social media.
It seems like their whole life is stored on one device,
But it's not really.

Staring at little rectangular screens of light,
People get completely obsessed and addicted.
Never a chance to go out to play,
And never a chance to see the day.
T.E.C.H.N.O.L.O.G.Y.
All together spells technology.

Chloe Chan (12)
Royal Wootton Bassett Academy, Swindon

SUMMER

Wind so humid and grass so green.
An ice cream man selling all his ice cream.
Children in paddling pools.
You feel like you're gonna pour one hundred ice cubes all over you so
you cool down.
Now every morning in your bed, wonder inside your head
Why you love summer.

Lewis Ablett-Jackson (11)
Royal Wootton Bassett Academy, Swindon

123

ENCLOSURE

I can see it there,
A great wall of hatred,
Blocking out all love from the things enclosed,
Happiness and Blessing cannot break through,
An impenetrable fortress penning me in.

Death's sick perfume lingers in the air,
Entering every lung and chest,
Suffocating, choking, killing,
There is no way out of this dark cave of sorrow,
We will stay here, every hope of escape snapped.

But a glimmer of hope pierces these walls,
I see it lying on a table,
Discarded, disregarded, shunned from existence,
Just a few pages with just a few words,
Bring me hope, a wonderful thing.

In books I see a new world,
One outside these impeding walls,
Where the sun pours down her rays of goodness,
This is the place where I find refuge,
There is no better place than my imagination.

Benjamin Coombs (13)
Royal Wootton Bassett Academy, Swindon

MY DOG

Maggie is my dog,
She likes to run in a fog,
She always likes to bark,
Especially when dark,
She likes to chew our shoes,
While looking upon a view.

Taylor Janine Anstee (11)
Royal Wootton Bassett Academy, Swindon

THE FIGHT FOR HUMAN RIGHTS

I am not afraid of your action,
Bombing our homes,
That causes a reaction.

Attacking us and our culture,
Coming at us like a vulture,
Hurting us all,
That's what we call.

Our hearts drowning,
In sadness of what we fear,
What will they do next
Or what will we hear?

Your crazy mind,
Starting to be kind,
But still punishing us,
For what we discuss.

So leave us alone,
And stop bombing our homes,
Never come back
Or we will hurt you back.

Millie Swift (12)
Royal Wootton Bassett Academy, Swindon

THE DOOR

Mysterious, intriguing,
How it just emerged
It beckoned me to open it
It delivers the feeling of desire.

What could lie behind it?
Possibly worlds covered in blue skies,
Children's giggles and smiles
Or a world of misery,
Sodden world full of discontent.

Cindy Namata (11)
Royal Wootton Bassett Academy, Swindon

125

RUGBY

The wonderful sport.
Perusing and devouring through the menu,
We're now excited to get to the venue.

Hustle, bustle, sights, sounds,
Showing our tickets to enter the ground.
Supporters jostling through turnstiles in their throngs,
Joking together, singing their songs.

Both sides in their kits, worn with pride,
On the pitch, there's nowhere to hide.

Whistle blown, kick-off commences,
Nerves shown by both defences.

Ruck, ruck, scrum, line out,
In the corner, 'Try!' They shout!

Highs, lows, cheers, cries,
Disbelief in everyone's eyes.

Hustle, bustle, sights, sounds,
The end upon us, exit the ground.

Jack John (12)
Royal Wootton Bassett Academy, Swindon

THE SECRET

Under the tree lies the secret,
Lying there,
Hoping to be found,
How long will it be there,
How much longer will it be there,
It will be there forever,
Unless the secret is shown,
Lots of times it will be unseen,
Until the right person
Is found.

Michael Redmond (11)
Royal Wootton Bassett Academy, Swindon

THE REAL HEROES

I sat in my great-grandad's sitting room
staring at the many awe-inspiring pictures and paintings
of Hurricanes and Spitfires.

I start to imagine the sound of their mighty engines roaring,
I start to imagine watching them defend Britain from the German
Luftwaffe
But then I also imagine working in factories
hearing the sound of a hammer hitting metal
wiping my brow because of the heat
the air thick with the smell of fire and oil.

I also imagine working at a radar centre
sending the word to the Air Force bases that the Luftwaffe were
coming.
I imagine watching the mighty planes taking off and flying into the
sky.

I then start to think of my great-grandad and all of his friends
They are real heroes.

Charlotte Tubb (15)
Royal Wootton Bassett Academy, Swindon

THE STORY OF SNOW WHITE

Snow White is the prettiest girl in the kingdom.
Her stepmother is the queen with the mystic mirror of the wood.
She seeks the response by questioning it,
'Mirror, mirror on the desk, who is the prettiest?'
Once she went into the woods and met some munchkins,
They took her in.
Her stepmother found out, she took some potion which turned her
old,
She poisoned the fruit, it killed Snow White.
The prince gave her kisses
Then they lived joyfully together forever.

Emily Joy Rogers (11)
Royal Wootton Bassett Academy, Swindon

A JOURNEY HOME

As the day came to an end,
The excited fish came round a bend.
He was not aware of what he would find
However he didn't stop or look behind.

In front of his eyes he could see,
A vast expanse of coral spreading as wide as can be.
His circular eyes lit up and shone,
All his sadness was begone.

Swimming around the colourful coral
He found two lobsters having a quarrel.
He ignored them, not giving a damn,
He continued swimming, he swam and swam.

He came to a familiar tunnel,
It started to become smaller, like a funnel.
Inside he knew what was waiting,
His whole family, their moods inflating.

Poppy Turner (12)
Royal Wootton Bassett Academy, Swindon

ZOO

I was on my way
Going by a zoo
When my dad opened the window
And suddenly bellowed boo!

I said, 'Look at all five monkeys
Lying like a family
How adorable do they look
Aww! One baby is called Amilee.'

Now I'm leaving Windsor Zoo,
I have to say goodbye
As we drive away
Finally see a small dove fly.

Susanne Cohen (11)
Royal Wootton Bassett Academy, Swindon

THE PENGUIN SLIDE

Slip, *slide*, *slippity*, *slide*, goes the penguin down the icy arctic slide.
He jumps and bumps into his friends hoping they can ride the slide.
The immeasurable glacier steepens and the penguin's zooming speed rises.

Slip, *slide*, *slippity*, *slide*, the penguin keeps on riding.
Suddenly an icicle falls, piercing his rubbery fin
However he keeps on sliding.

He sees a friend who holds his hand,
They rise off together,
They worry about their home of ice due to the sunny weather.
Slip,slide, slippity, slide.

Slip, *slide*, *slippity*, *slide*, goes the penguin down the icy arctic slide.
The immeasurable glacier steepens and the penguin's zooming speed rises.
So fast the penguin flies.

Samuel Owen Wynne Jackson (12)
Royal Wootton Bassett Academy, Swindon

THE DISMAL DAY

The bitter breeze blew into the atmosphere,
Trees wept with their usual melancholic tone,
And the wind howled with its usual sense of sadness.
The expanse was so deserted even the bench was alone.

Continuous blowing echoed in the distance,
The eerie moon lay up in the sky,
The day will never end,
The truth stays far away, all you can hear is a lie.

Happy memories are unimaginable,
Here in this dismal place,
The sky is never blue and the sun never comes out,
When I see your dismal face.

Amy Hadfield
Royal Wootton Bassett Academy, Swindon

DRESSAGE

Soft, yellow under the horses feet,
in the hot sun they ride,
focusing the key to success,
their eyes on the prize, plus the ribbons,
both bodies pounding, needing to win.
Will they?

Twirling slowly in perfect circles,
prettifying the whole competition,
every move counts to winning,
pictures fill their heads,
of riding in the woods together.
Lots of fun, they did it, they won!

Holly Sweeby (11)
Royal Wootton Bassett Academy, Swindon

LONG AGO, FAR AWAY...

Tears fall, ashes fade,
long ago, memories made,
poppies wither, leaves burn,
bones sharpen, stomachs churn,
wind howls, stones weight,
moon falls, fingers grate,
shadows whisper, trees crowd,
screams echo, bodies shroud,
hearts stop, pain slashes,
bloody hands, burnt gashes,
a world so sombre, yet full of light,
falls gently into that painless night.

Finley Isabelle Delooze (13)
Royal Wootton Bassett Academy, Swindon

THE SWAP

Tell me, why are you blue?
You wouldn't understand, you're just human.
Just tell me, what do you want?
Your happiness, love, friendship, family, companionship.
You can have mine, but I want something in return!
What?
Your treasure; diamonds, rubies, gold, silver, oh I want it, give it to me!
Agreed, fool, I will spend my life happy.
I will spend my life guarding my treasure.

Lucy Blackmur (13)
Royal Wootton Bassett Academy, Swindon

TIGERS IN THE ZOO

Stuck behind steel poles,
Hiding from the living things,
Suddenly, two tiny eyes emerge,
Then the rest of the tiger strolls in.

She's got sooty stripes
With her tummy coloured like cheese puffs.
Dusk comes, no living things,
On the prowl, behind steel poles,
Lurks a heroic tiger in a zoo.

Charlotte Alice Bullock (11)
Royal Wootton Bassett Academy, Swindon

AUTUMN DAYS

The wind whistles quietly
Whilst red with yellow puddles swirl round the huge trees.

The mornings look windy but composed.
It is forever crisp with gloomy skies.

Conkers of shiny brown drift onto the colourful ground.
Bright red swirls in the sky.

The children do competitions
Where they kick the puddles of golden yellow.

Isabella Draycott (11)
Royal Wootton Bassett Academy, Swindon

DREAMS

A new life, a sandy dream
Any dream can happen filled with magic beings
A land of colours
A life following dark in a world of gleaming sun,
Rainbows, unicorns and sun
Dreams are inspiring.

Charley Wilmott (11)
Royal Wootton Bassett Academy, Swindon

HORRIBLE THOUGHTS

The red walls and horrid memories were permanently in my mind;
Screeching sounds and ugly thoughts surrounded my entire presence,
Happy nights and sweet friends were no longer imaginable,
All these things were replaced with regretful mistakes
and sorrowful memories dancing in my mind.

Tannaz Hooshyarabnavi (13)
Royal Wootton Bassett Academy, Swindon

THE MIRROR REFLECTION

An imaginary pathway to wondrous splendour
A place you can love, learn and discover
Like a dove unchained be free, fly away
Flecks of gold and sparks of silver,
You're an individual sun in a colossal galaxy.

Louise Mwihia (11)
Royal Wootton Bassett Academy, Swindon

ALIEN

A ll green
L aughing in a dark zone
I n an endless sky
E arly in a morning
N ever seen before.

Nathan White (11)
Royal Wootton Bassett Academy, Swindon

THE AMAZON FOREST

When night arrives, the dense rainforest turns alive,
The weather is always a mystery in the Amazon sky.
Open water waves, break at the shoreline.
Mosquitoes flutter, birds sing, the trees open to let the sun shine in.

Maddie Jones (11)
Royal Wootton Bassett Academy, Swindon

CUTE AND CUDDLY PUPPIES

Puppies are cute and cuddly
They will be cute unless you leave a puppy on the sofa
Puppies need a lot of care
Let them have freedom and a lot of walks
Make them have a safe and lovely life
Never abandon a lost dog, care for it and take it to the vets
Make you and your pets as safe as you possibly can.

Joanna Kusznerko (11)
St Augustine's Catholic College, Trowbridge

BEGINNING TO THE END

The earth as cold as ice and dark as hell
Boom! What was that? A terrestrial planet was made
How lovely is that?
The animal was manufactured by God
Trees, plants, sea, ocean was created
All of this for who?
He made humans, us!
We lived in earth for billions of years in peace
Then we started, started fighting
Eleven countries fought to regain peace
What was the meaning for all of this?
We fought, we fought then . . . we won, peace at last, but it wasn't
over yet
Couple of years . . . it began again
Thirteen countries fought again
Fought and fought, will it be over?
Five years fighting agitated.

We won again,
Finally at peace, or is it?
We made an agreement, no war, no fighting
So peace at last, with peacefulness we live longer than before
We live, we live, not all of us now
Middle East, what's happening?
People dying, why?
Let's save them by giving donations
Don't ignore them,
Don't think it's not your business cause it is
It stops peace for all and all shall never do this again
Peace, peace, and peace until one day the world will come to an end
An end to all things starts small, gradually grows big
Then the end and all shall live in Heaven, in peace.

Albi Jinson (11)
St Augustine's Catholic College, Trowbridge

CHASER OF LIGHT

I chased the light,
Bright through the night,
Till rays of dawn,
Did morning yawn.

Went left, went right,
For chaser's plight,
But I was strong,
And I held on.

Grappled and grabbed,
Then did my hand,
Touch the whispers,
Soft and crisper.

A twist, a shout,
A moment of doubt,
Light in my hands,
Shrinks and expands.

Stood still, silent,
Moment triumph,
Then slow, but sure,
The light was no more.

The touch was all,
The touch was small,
I yearned for more,
It's gone, for sure!

Tried my hardest,
For memories,
The slightest!
But the light was gone,
Oh how I longed!

Stood lost and cold,
But no more gold,
Did dip and dive,
Forever mine.

Moment of woe,
Then the glow,

Did dip and dive,
Before my eyes.

Tightly I held,
Too tight I held,
The light seeped through,
The golden hue!

It ran away,
To fading day,
To be with the sun,
And I did run.

I chased the light,
Bright through the night,
Till rays of dawn,
Did morning yawn . . .

Mary Elizabeth Haine (13)
St Augustine's Catholic College, Trowbridge

FIRE

The lights go out, the house is filled with darkness for the night or is it?
A young man wearing anger on his face picks up the small box of matches then opens it
He examines the solitary match then *scratch* and *pop*, the match ignites
A very small and gentle flame burns quietly on the match
The angry man tosses the match on the floor and the fire begins to grow
As it grows it gets angry and swallows its creator.
It violently burns through the building
Burning away the blanket of darkness, leaving a trail of yellow, orange and red
It eventually engulfs the whole building making bright light shine through the garden
The fire is popping and cracking. It laughs as the people watch it burn.

Daniel Marchese (12)
St Augustine's Catholic College, Trowbridge

INDESTRUCTIBLE BY VOW

The time has come for me
It's the time I will drown in the river of fear
I will go to the bottom of the sea of anger which is as hot as molten
despair
My skin is burnt
But it does not hurt
I will never die
I'm un-killable
I will never ever die
But I will rise like a phoenix from the ashes of hatred
I will break the barrier of death and life
And no one will stop me
No one will ever destroy me
You try and you will be destroyed
Like all the others
You think I'm mad
But I'm not
I just want people to feel what I feel
You want to know what I felt
I felt sad and scared

Lonely and heartbroken
Burned to death, I drowned
Un-seeable by happiness
But seeable by fear
I'm dead
I'm dead like a volcano that died
I think of everyone as demons who they are
I'm not saying that I'm good but what they did to me is
Cruel, evil, irresponsible
Like death, they take life from me
I was born to end the . . . the world.

Oliwier Maziarski (12)
St Augustine's Catholic College, Trowbridge

LIGHT

Sunlight, sunshine, glowing brightly up there
Beautiful and golden, you warm up the air
Butterflies and fireflies fluttering to the sky
Their little wings flap graciously until they're up high
Then down they all come, prettier than ever
And give me a little gift of sunlight forever.

I hold it carefully in my hands
It's silky smooth, and just like sand
It runs through my fingers ever so slowly
It's warm, it glows, it twinkles, it burns
And smells delicious and heavenly
Flowing into a special jar of mine
Humming quietly, it fills my ears with glee.

Just like a fairy tale's golden hand
It glitters and shines and makes you smile
And all the while
Giving you dreams
It touches a child to giggle in sleep
With every turn and every touch
It makes something out there right and just.

But eventually I must let go,
To walk to the sea and bend down low
I pour it gently out the jar
It spreads through the sea as quick as can be
Filling the sky with a shine so bright
It swirls and twirls and disappears
A golden mist rising slowly through the air.

Daniella Billington (13)
St Augustine's Catholic College, Trowbridge

THE IDEA BLOCK

Oh no!
Oh Jeez!
I've decided to write a poem,
But I don't know what to type!
A flying duck
A singing trout!
I really don't have a clue,
I could write about:
The sky,
The sea,
Oh, I really need some inspiration!
The dirt,
The grass,
I expect people feel commiseration!
The birds,
The panes,
Tick-tock, tick-tock,
I know!
I'll get an idea block!
It'll give me inspiration,
So people won't feel commiseration,
It'll make me feel proud,
That I can finally be loud,
By expressing my excitement,
Wait!
I know!
I'll write against the clock.
About the idea block!

Paige MacDonald (12)
St Augustine's Catholic College, Trowbridge

MY LIGHT CREATION

If I was to catch sunlight,
I would fly in a large space rocket with a dangerous blaze of fire
I would fly up through the night,
And every second getting higher and higher
Getting ever closer to the ignition of the glowing sunlight.
I would float down to Earth,
Hoping not to burn up in the atmosphere
Or even crash in Perth,
To just land safely in the sphere
With my joyful sunlight right here.
I would go back to my lab,
And create something just fab.

Once I finished my creation,
I pour the sloppy liquid into my hands,
It is something for the nation.
After months and years of plans
All I could smell was burnt toast,
Even at night when I was in my space rocket,
I tried to put it in a letter for the post,
But to my creation I kept applying,
To make it better and better.

I wish I could fly,
I wish I could see the night sky,
All I want to be is out there,
Not to just throw a flare,
In the night sky,
I just want to fly.

Tom Stephens (14)
St Augustine's Catholic College, Trowbridge

A CAT OF TWO LIVES

Just centimetres away
Will she be successful?
Almost cross-eyed
She will get her pride
How does she do it?
Every time she proves it

The poor creature has no clue
When she comes for food

What was that?
What did I see?
A blink of an eye
A twitch of a flea

She licks her lips
Satisfied
Her eyes glimmering
I watch her, shivering

But she looks so innocent
Standing there
She looks at me
Eyes full of mischief
She agrees

Dozing there without a care
Stretching out, no sign of scare
No energy today . . .
Is this the same cat I saw yesterday?

Yasmin Zuzia Kaczorek (12)
St Augustine's Catholic College, Trowbridge

WHAT IF I STOLE LIGHT?

What if I stole light?
What if I made everything dark?
What if it was no longer bright?
Would cats begin to howl and bark?
Would teddy bears become the monsters of the night?
I wonder what would happen if I stole light?

Would the world go topsy-turvy?
Would rules become curvy?
Would teachers be taught by students?
Would recycling become pollutants?
Would policemen encourage a fight?
I wonder what would happen if I stole light?

What if it became completely dark?
Would the world be ruled by a shark?
Would humans stumble about
Or would we just chill out?
Would a match ignite?
I wonder what would happen if I stole the light?

What if it was permanently night?
Would we be deprived of sight?
What would happen to solar energy?
Would Bear Grylls become a veggie?
Would people still stay overnight?
I think I like the idea
Of stealing light.

Ed Nightingale (13)
St Augustine's Catholic College, Trowbridge

BATTLING DARKNESS

As the lightning struck,
I was ready with a jar,
Chasing it for days,
I had travelled very far.

Trickling over darkness,
I was spreading joy.
Everywhere that needed help,
To every girl and boy.

It flowed slow and steady,
Like honey from a hive.
I must not waste all of it,
It keeps all joy alive.

Pouring out the last drops,
In an old, abandoned house.
My final gift of happiness,
My fire being doused.

Join me in the battle,
Of good against bad.
If darkness does take over,
The whole world will be sad.

Some day I wish I could catch some more,
The lightning that brought joy.
I could donate my gift to the world again,
To every girl and boy . . .

Roan Jeffery (13)
St Augustine's Catholic College, Trowbridge

FIRE

The light is blinding,
Burning everything in its path.
It leaps at you,
Viciously striking.

As hot as the sun,
As wild as a tiger.
As destructive as a weapon
As beautiful as a flower.

Danger, dressed as love.
Amazing but lethal.
Hotter and louder,
The more it is fed.

Living off food alone,
Water making it powerless.
Draining all energy,
From the deadly beast.

It dwells in the corner,
Trapped in one place.
Guarded and controlled,
No longer a threat.

No longer a beast,
No longer a danger.
Now a source of comfort,
And a beacon of light.

Matthew O'Connell (14)
St Augustine's Catholic College, Trowbridge

THE RAY OF SUNLIGHT

The single ray of sunlight,
bright and bold for all to see,
quickly darted through the air
and stopped in front of me

The single ray of sunlight,
as quickly as it came.
Danced around my room and stopped,
Zap! It was gone again.

The single ray of sunlight,
that had fallen from the sky;
reappeared later that evening
and around my bedroom ceiling it began to fly.

The single ray of sunlight
stopped and with a whistling sound,
fell through the air like honey
and transformed into a powder when it hit the ground.

I cupped the glowing powder in my hands
and the world around me seemed to glow,
and with this powder in my hands
to the darkest corners of the world I will go

With the sunlight in my hands
far and wide I will soar
and where the world seems cold and bleak
the sunlight I will pour

Shiku Ogborn (13)
St Augustine's Catholic College, Trowbridge

DANGEROUS, DEADLY, DESTRUCTIVE

I engulf everything,
Everything I touch,
It's all against my will.
I don't want to do this.
Take people's lives away,
But I cannot stop.

I wish I could stop the screaming
I wish I could stop the pain
I wish I could stop the crying,
And all the pain I have caused
By burning and killing
As I immerse everything I see,
People run and try to flee
As they turn round
I see myself in their eyes
Scarlet, orange, yellow and gold.
Dangerous, deadly, destructive.
I reach out one hand
Out towards them
I hear a blood-curdling scream
And they're gone.

Lucja Jadwiga Korczak (12)
St Augustine's Catholic College, Trowbridge

I WISH YOU WERE HERE

The moment that you died I felt my heart break in two
One was grieving you, the other died with you
I remember at your funeral holding Mother's hand
We wept, we cried but still we carried on
We all wore yellow to try and make life colourful
But yet it could not hide the grieving we felt inside.
Time passed on and you were not forgotten
Each day I went and prayed for you
In hope you were all right up there
We made a book in memory of you and placed it on your chair
We all looked through it one by one
With tears down our cheeks we took a walk down memory lane
That day we went and cleared your flat of everything you had
But still keeping hold of all the precious things you kept
When we left the room I turned back to take a look
And in the corner of the room I swear I saw you there
Standing by the window waving me goodbye
And you whispered in my ear, 'I'm always with you in your heart.'
With tears in my eyes I left and locked the door, wishing you were there.
Now I know that you are up there in the sky watching down on me
I hope that when my time comes you will be up there watching, waiting for me.

Harriet Maria Lemay-Lamb (12)
St Augustine's Catholic College, Trowbridge

LIFE'S TRUE TREASURE

Vanishing slowly behind the world we know,
Guiding us on life's exciting journey,
Like a mighty angel,
Lighting up only the true,
Ignited by love,
Light shows us the way.

Freddie Stoddart (13)
St Augustine's Catholic College, Trowbridge

AEIPATHY OF FIRE

I feast on the darkness, on the darkness of the outside and in
A stolen kiss from the dulling flames of death
A graceful arabesque of flames, watch it and smile as the world burns
Hatred glowing brighter than love
Dance to the sound of screams
Laugh until your throat pleads
Let me show you how fire works
Gold, blue and crimson red
Held gently on a candle until it bleeds
Forced onto a firework until it screams
Trapped in a lantern until it gleams
Concealing itself until the epitome of rage breaks through
Addicted to the melody of crackling
Humming along the way you would to a lullaby
Sing the night into silence
Your life is an accepted sacrifice
So let me show you how fire works
Clinquant looks, don't judge a book by its cover
Caressing your fingertips, everything resonating to non-existing
Breathe ragged, experiment in session
Danger, excitement, drifts into the abyss
Let me show you how fire dies.

Kelly Ifechukwu Ibenegbu (12)
St Augustine's Catholic College, Trowbridge

DARKNESS

When the darkness falls, with
No more problems that the light had brought,
The bitter frost makes my body shudder.
The city lights make my eyes feel numb;
A rustle and a crunch ...
Invisible leaves under my invisible boots;
A glimmer from the stars shines through the branches;
The moon is my spotlight and I am its actor.

Tallulah Richards (13)
St Augustine's Catholic College, Trowbridge

EMBRACE THE LIGHT

I glitter and glisten,
To make you listen.
With all my power,
You can bloom a flower.

Embrace the light,
With all your might.
I help you do fractions,
I can help you do refraction.

I tumble and turn against time,
Excruciating, heated distances through circuits.
I race against everything.
To make all things brighter.

Let me come in,
Let me shine in you,
Like a lightning bug,
Your heart will glow.

Grab the light,
Trap the light,
So kids, what I'm saying is . . .
Once I'm gone,
I'm gone.

Senuri Alwis (13)
St Augustine's Catholic College, Trowbridge

FADED

I was in a room,
Hundreds of people around me.
I felt alone.
Like the light inside of me had faded.

Darkness filled me,
I heard not a sound,
People passing by me.
I fell to the ground.

The lights started to dim,
Flickering all around.
The light I used to see brightly
Left me scared and anxious.

People gathered to check I was fine,
I responded with silence.
I slowly shut my eyelids.
Then I woke up seeing light.

This time it was different.
I didn't feel terrified.
I now see light may dim
But always comes back bright.

Niamh Day (13)
St Augustine's Catholic College, Trowbridge

CAPTURING SUNLIGHT

I caught the sunlight in a jar,
It did not come from very far,
From a forest where the sunlight shines,
From the treetops, it is now mine.

I poured the sunlight into my hands,
It dripped and I watched it expand,
Smelling like lemon and autumn leaves,
Just like honey, it drizzled down free.

I have the power to touch anything,
I have no idea where to go,
I shall travel to many places,
And turn various objects into gold.

It glows and glitters and,
Shines so gorgeously and,
At night, it's brighter than the moon,
It's warm and beautiful, I forget about any gloom.

I caught the sunlight in a jar,
It did not come from very far,
From a forest where the sunlight shines,
From the treetops, it is now mine.

Samantha Box (13)
St Augustine's Catholic College, Trowbridge

FIREWORK

I am shining joy,
The biggest star,
The child's dream.

I am the raging red,
The burning blue,
The glittering green.

I am the biggest *bang*,
The loudest *crack*,
The rolling *boom*.

I am the crackling fire,
The sizzling sausages,
Ready soon.

I am the fastest flyer,
The feeling-changer,
The spreader of light.

I am the fleeing sparrows,
The tallest mountain,
Lost into the night.

I am, I am, I am.

Alexandra Rossiter (12)
St Augustine's Catholic College, Trowbridge

IF LIGHT WERE HUMAN

The sun would dream of singing softly with the stars as they gradually grow distant.
A light bulb would talk about the calmness of hanging helplessly and being blown by the breeze.
Fire talks of death and destruction, and being capable of turning cities to ash as it gradually erodes the pile of coal hungrily.
Lightning would dream of striking Earth, catching small glimpses of its beauty.
Torches would dream of fear, catching glimpses of its surroundings, as it darts from left to right.
Candles would dream of nightmarish scenarios, getting its bearings and finding unknown creatures . . .
A firework would wear silk, fine and bright clothing, as it dances in the moonlight.
Lanterns would talk of hands clamping around them and sudden confusion as they are hauled over into the darkness.
Glow sticks would wear bright stunning clothes as they illuminate the darkness.
Headlights would talk of long, perilous journeys across deserted terrain.

Thomas Bennett (11)
St Augustine's Catholic College, Trowbridge

A SPARKLER IN THE DARK

I bring joy to those who hold me
My orange yellow heart, grows and grows with
Little sparkles flickering in the dark.
I crackle and spit as I run down the stick
Still carrying my little glow.
Although I only last a quick minute or two
I've spent my life making footprints on some hearts.
I am what I am, an orange little spark,
A sparkler in the dark!

Gabriella Eve Doel (12)
St Augustine's Catholic College, Trowbridge

LIGHT

The sun rises and sets like a gigantic enlightened copper coin being lowered or lifted,
Sometimes you can see it, sometimes you can't, because of the cotton wool-like clouds,
At night you can only see the moon, but the sun is really the brightest star,
When the blazing hot sun is shining, people are usually smiling.

Sunglasses, paddling pools, sun lotion and laughter, all make a happy holiday in the shining sun,
The scorching sun makes everything bright,
But the really, really bright sun, can also blind because it is so bright,
So safety should always be the highest priority.

The flaming sun brings joy to all because, in the sunlight, you always feel warm,
The shining sun makes you feel much safer than if you were in a storm,
I just love being cosy and warm in the glowing sun,
The light and warmth of the sun makes people want to sunbathe and relax all day.

Elijah Michael Joseph Wilson (11)
St Augustine's Catholic College, Trowbridge

SYMPTOMS OF SUICIDE

Don't leave the home
Everyone laughs at him/her
Always crying
Death awaits them . . .

If you see them with symptoms help them
Or the final symptom will occur after death awaits them . . .

Scare away the bullies teasing them about their hair
And whatever you do, don't leave them in despair . . .

Katie Mortimer Jenkins (11)
St Augustine's Catholic College, Trowbridge

IMAGINE YOU COULD CATCH SUNLIGHT IN A JAR...

Imagine you could catch sunlight in a jar . . .
It would shine bright all day and all night.
You could see it shining and glowing from miles
Glistening bright with everlasting love.

It would pour and pour into the hands,
As if it was hot and tropical sand.
The orange and lime smell would warm you up,
And it would glitter and glitter all night.

Imagine you could catch sunlight in a jar . . .
Everything it touches starts shining and glowing.
The light would bring back many memories,
And it would make all the wishes come true.

The light would shine bright like a halo, at night,
It would illuminate, shine, glitter and sparkle
So just imagine right now,
Imagine you could catch sunlight in a jar.

Urszula Kalinowska (13)
St Augustine's Catholic College, Trowbridge

WHAT IF?

What if I never saw the sun?
What if I had no heart?
What if I could never love?

What if I bit into an apple and blood dripped out on the ground?
What if I lived in a lonely corner with no one to help?
What if every time someone cries the ground shakes?

What if this is all a dream and we are not real?
What if you lost your friend for ever?

What if everything you loved vanished
Into nowhere?

Gabrielle Ann Sturdee (11)
St Augustine's Catholic College, Trowbridge

THE LIGHT AS YOU MAY NOT KNOW IT

Light is immortal. It can form anything.
Light soars down like an eagle and glistens on the water.
Light battles with darkness and illuminates the world.
Light can be friend or foe.
Light can be an angry teenager, blazing with fire;
Or a peaceful baby with a heavenly halo.
Light can be a scientist full of questions and answers
Light can be a prison cell with dark feelings and rage *lashing* out.
Light can be human eyes, a guardian through life
Light can be an escape to your desires and dreams
Light can be beautiful
Light can be dreadful
Light can be nothing but awe and wonder.
Light can be thunder,
Light can be the moon,
Light can be the sun.
Light, I can never hide, I can never run . . .

Malcolm Ibenegbu (13)
St Augustine's Catholic College, Trowbridge

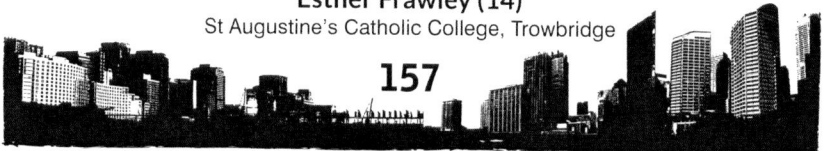

THE LIGHT OF LIFE

Glistening shapes of light shine above me,
I trap it with my grasp.
Light dances around my face like fireworks exploding – a rainbow.
Light is warm, light is cold, light is the sight in your eyes,
Light is like a trap, light is clear.
It is the reflection of the truth.

The light absorbs peace so we are all free.
Now it's night but the light of the moon is complete.
A star is a captured dot of light in the sky.
So light is a sparkle in your eye.
Light is near but impossible to reach.

Esther Frawley (14)
St Augustine's Catholic College, Trowbridge

YoungWriters

BLINDING SUNLIGHT

Sunlight.
It shines the brightest in the dark of the lights.
The mech I put on, very tight.
I can see all of the world and its sights.
Powered by sunlight, it rests.
Sitting safely in the centre of my chest.
Glittery and smooth.
It warms the suit.
And flashes rapidly.
It gives off a spark.
Bites like a shark.
It powers it up.
Shaping into a cup.
When used, it flashes a ray.
Which nearly makes it fray.
And then makes everyone say:
'Wow, what a delight!'
Sunlight.

Jack Rodrigues (13)
St Augustine's Catholic College, Trowbridge

LIGHT BEAMS

Light beams down on the highest peaks of mountains
Flowing down in waves,
Engulfing forests and blinding the shadows
Filling all untouched spaces,
Exposed all the grand views.
Light beams on the dancing stars,
Illuminating the twilight sky
Radiating their magnificent rays,
Flashing intense colours
On the sleeping towns.
Light beams on everything.

Maddie Green (13)
St Augustine's Catholic College, Trowbridge

CONSCIOUS

In every star that glimmers bright,
Are wishes with glints of hope.
No matter how dark the world becomes,
There will be dreams of warped light.

On and on the gentle light will glow,
Locked, chained inside our hearts.
Some stained with fear and rage,
But the light will never fade.

We are the luminous light,
Creating our own paths.
Engraving our footsteps,
Reaching out to the unknown.

We are birds of light,
Freed from our cages,
Flying from the binding darkness,
Flying, from our sins.

Tilly Jones (13)
St Augustine's Catholic College, Trowbridge

LIGHT AND DARK

I ignite in the dark
So you don't fear the night.
I will guide your way through,
I will keep you light.

I will be here,
Whether you need me or not;
I will stay by your side,
Through the cold and the hot.

It may just happen
That I slip out of your sight;
But I promise I'll be there
In the dark or the light.

Sophie Spencer-Brown (13)
St Augustine's Catholic College, Trowbridge

THE GIFT

The great white cloak,
and a very old bloke,
when he came to me,
he sat me down to tea.

We went outside,
to find a surprise,
of darkness around May,
his calmness went away.

He waved about,
in a shout,
and darkness withdrew itself,
we continued until we met an elf.

It hopped and skipped with joy,
when he gave it a new toy,
his gift was a chance to see,
when I grow up, that's who I want to be.

Matthew Joseph Edward Wiltshire (13)
St Augustine's Catholic College, Trowbridge

IF LIGHT WERE HUMAN

The moon says, 'sweet dreams' to the world,
The sun turns off her lights,
The stars wish that they could be seen.

Neon signs direct the night like a conductor,
Neon bands party through the night.

The light bulb dreams about brightening everyone's day,
A candle dreams of being strong,
The fire spreads warmth across our hearts.

Lightning crashes down on the Earth in rage,
The warmth of the sun protects us,
The moon puts the Earth to bed.

Blubell Walker (11)
St Augustine's Catholic College, Trowbridge

FAIRY LIGHTS

I can be red,
I can be blue.
I can be big,
Or small too.
Hang me in your room,
Or on your Christmas tree.
Wherever you choose to put me,
Make sure I can be seen!

I have many good neighbours,
On my left and on my right.
When our switch is flicked on,
Oh, what a beautiful sight!

But when it comes to that time when you shut your eyes,
And you've all had your lovely mince pies,
And the jolly Christmas atmosphere dies,
Then it's time for us fairy lights to say our goodbyes.

Mair Edwards Williams (12)
St Augustine's Catholic College, Trowbridge

TEN THINGS A RANDOM OLD LADY HAS IN HER POCKET

1 A dead body
2 A bloody hand
3 Poison
4 A bird head pie
5 A fat cat.
6 A dead rat.
7 A knife.
8 A gun
9 Bullets
10 A broom.

Is she as random as we thought?

Laura Klucinska (11)
St Augustine's Catholic College, Trowbridge

IF LIGHT WAS HUMAN

If light was human,
Stars would feel exuberant when people turn and stare.
Lightning would feel sad when people run and hide.
Fireworks would tell a story when they burst high in the sky.
Disco lights would move like a leaf flying down the street.
Fire will remember its disappearing life as coals turn into ashes.
If light was human.

If light was human,
The sun would wish that his loneliness would fade.
A candle would think a flicker could change everything.
Computer screens would wait for games to appear and bring
happiness.
Electricity would run to win the race.
Sparks would dream of being let free and whizzing around the pitch-
black sky.
If light was human.

Millie Harriet Lewis (11)
St Augustine's Catholic College, Trowbridge

FIREFLIES

A glitter,
A shimmer,
A flicker . . .
Illuminating the skin on my palm,
Holding the intense light in my visible darkness.
A twinkle,
A sparkle,
A glisten . . .
But many. They're lurking.
Tails on fire with a flash of light.
A jar
A jar
Of fireflies.

Megan Watts (13)
St Augustine's Catholic College, Trowbridge

IF LIGHT WERE HUMAN...

Lava would moan about how he turned everything he touched into ashes,
Fire would remember the time he almost burnt London to the ground,
A firework would dream about shooting up into space and transforming into stars, where people would look at him for ever.
Lightning would smell like a mixture of a fry-up and singed clothing.
The moon would shed tears as she thought of the companions she never had,
A lantern would imagine leading the biggest expedition in the world,
A torch's favourite hobby would be casting shadow puppets on a wall,
A sparkler would dream of burning as brightly as the sun,
The stars would be proud of the comfort they bring,
Because for some, seeing the stars is a pleasure,
A TV would hum as softly as an electric fence.

Maeve Ellis (11)
St Augustine's Catholic College, Trowbridge

SHROUDING LIGHT

Sometimes, I think I see lights,
In the distance, far away
Too far, to even comprehend, to hold.
Oh how I yearn to grasp,
to feel the warm caress of hope
on my war-battered hands.
It is the light that keeps me going,
that stops me from toppling in the dark storm,
even though the inevitability of oblivion
stalks the halls of my soul.
It is the light that stops the questions,
the endless lamenting queries about the meaning of all this
drilling their way slowly, tauntingly into my heart . . .
Oh how I yearn for the light.

Sam Ridley (14)
St Augustine's Catholic College, Trowbridge

IF LIGHT WAS HUMAN

Sparklers would whisper words of calming,
The sun would smell of sweet sulphur and burnt gas,
Fireworks would remember when they were separated from their family,
Glow bands would feel exuberant when they are cracked,
Phones would sing when they are happy,
Aurora Borealis would yearn for a season ticket,
Fire would dance at sundown with its many jolly friends,
Candles would wish they were immortal,
Torches would remember when they were switched on, died and dumped,
Chinese lanterns would visit far away back gardens,
Lightning would always favour the tallest,
Stars would glide across the moonlit silky sea,
Phosphorescence would disappear with a wave of a magician's wand,
LEDs would outwit the smartest of ideas!

Sam Robert Goddard (11)
St Augustine's Catholic College, Trowbridge

SPARKLER

I sparkle like a glittery dress under the sun.
I am gold, yellow and orange.
My sound is a *fizz* like oil on a hot pan.
My smell a wonderful smell, I smell like fire.
When I am touched I feel happiness and joy
But yet inside I am angry, full of rage and I don't know why.
When people see me they are happy, full of joy.
I move quickly down my rod until I fizzle out
But then I am re-lit again and again, until I can be lit no more.
I see the world as a beautiful place, full of colour by day
And by night an inky blackness with the twinkle of the stars above.
I come out at night
I am a sparkler.

Catherine Yuill (12)
St Augustine's Catholic College, Trowbridge

CALMNESS

I am my own light,
I shine in the darkness to give hope.
I swiftly move around,
Bringing light everywhere.
I see the world through my soft flame,
I see good in everyone and everything.
I see people relax as they see and touch me in a dim-lit room.
I am my own light,
I shine in the darkness.
I am long and round,
The colour of a soft cream feather cushion.
I am quiet and calm,
All you can hear is my faint flickering of my breath.
I am my own light,
I shine in the darkness.

Aine A Jarvis (12)
St Augustine's Catholic College, Trowbridge

STARS

At night before bed
I open the window above my head.
A sea of stars, yes that's what I see.
A whole bunch smiling at me.
Flash!
A shooting star racing across the sky.
Nearly too fast for my eyes.
I made a wish and looked up again and
Prayed to the heavens and God again.
Now I'm happy as can be
Knowing God is looking down on me.

Maisie Hanlon (12)
St Augustine's Catholic College, Trowbridge

IF LIGHTS WERE HUMAN

The sun shouts down to the Earth with her song,
Candles dream of dancing through the woods,
Matches think of their friends, each a head filled with warmth,
A sparkler prancing through the coal-black night,
A torch, exploring the unknown when times are dark,
Computer screens whisper, wondering where their friends are in the
long cold days,
The light bulb swings wondering what her planet is like,
Fireworks remember the sadness of their brothers and sisters,
Lightning feels angry when times turn grey,
Glow sticks wear colourful cloaks, enjoying life.

Gabriel Longbotham
St Augustine's Catholic College, Trowbridge

WINTER WEATHER

Winter weather is coming towards us,
It makes the roads slimy and dangerous.
With it's dark clouds and heavy rain pouring,
And it gets worse when the snow is falling.
I would like drivers to take extra care,
By driving slowly and being aware.

Winter weather is sometimes exciting,
Snow angels, sledging and snowball fighting.
Wellingtons, hats and scarves must be worn,
But make sure your clothes don't get wet and torn.
Build a snowman family in the park,
Don't forget to go when it's spooky dark.

Winter weather can be wet, cold and bitter,
But it is always entertaining us!

Hannah Hart (13)
St Bede's Catholic College, Bristol

WINTER'S ROSE

Winter's rose lies upon the glistening snow,
Infinite beauty preserved as Winter's gift.
As Winter's reign gives its first blow,
Lying amongst crystals is the reddest of rubies

Sweet aroma of moist dew and rose perfume,
Floating gently in the ice cold breeze.
As crimson roses come into bloom,
Redder than love, innocent and enchanting.

Precious innocence young and pure,
Sweeter than the morning mist.
With an irresistible beauty that will lure,
Romantic, regal and radiant
Winter's rose.

Amy Rose Koikkara (12)
St Bede's Catholic College, Bristol

THE RUINED DAY OUT

Sand tingling down the tips of toes, blast of sand
Restlessly pushing towels
Daylight beginning to open into the sandy atmosphere.

Sea hitting the skin of the beach, umbrellas popping up
Like a Mexican wave
Children digging their parents into the sandy underworld.

Suddenly a gloomy storm comes howling, creeping up
Behind the blast of restless wind,
Bitter rain dancing round the flat flakes of sand snuffling to life.

A sudden howl roared and all was gone. There were no more echoes
All dead silent
The clouds sailed into the horizon and the sun shyly peeped out.

Shauna Camp-Sorensen (12)
St Mary's School, Shaftesbury

PONY POEM

I was cantering across a field,
Trying to do a leg yield?
I'm riding horse and hound,
I've got a clear round.

I will come first at Burghley,
It's all very girly.
Not!

I was racing in Kentucky
I was very, very lucky.

I'm at the Grand National,
It's all very rational.
I will ride at Blenheim,
I will fall in love with him.

One pony's called Rosie,
She's sometimes very dozy.
Another's called Bella,
She is my fella?

The second's called Poppy
Her strides are choppy.
The other is Sovereign,
And he's the king of heaven.

I've won the Triple Crown,
I've sent the others down.
I will not go to shame,
or I will not have my fame.

Penelope Aggett (12)
St Mary's School, Shaftesbury

FLAMES

I rise, cracking and spluttering,
Warming people to the bones;
I light the way for some,
But can drive others from their homes.

I can rampage through streets,
Causing terror and pain;
People lose their lives to me,
But I care not what I gain.

I can cook food for some,
The family's Sunday roast;
I can burn meat to ashes,
Or turn people into ghosts.

I can crawl through royal palaces,
Without regard for class;
I can leave my mark on people,
Licking their skin as I pass.

Yet once subdued and tamed,
I can help people heal;
I can warm their hearts and homes,
And give them their daily meal.

Poppy Wakefield (14)
St Mary's School, Shaftesbury

BOOMERANG

'What is a boomerang?' a little girl asked.
'I got it for my birthday and I am going to play.'

'A boomerang,' I exclaimed, 'the v-shaped sort?'
'Yes,' cried the little girl. 'It's time I made it swirl!'

'A boomerang,' I said, 'springs back as if it is scared of being caught in
the dainty spider web.'
A boomerang flicks and twists and curls in the sky.
It dances in the morning breeze.
It flies until it makes a U turn and bounces back.'

'Yes, thank you, but how do I throw it?'
'Splendid,' I cried. 'You hold it as if it was a hairbrush, and flick it into
the sky!'

She tried and tried and tried
Until owls called their midnight song.
Finally, the boomerang glided through the evening sky
Collecting the stars as they turned through the gentle wind.

Smiling, I said, 'The owls have sung and you need to go.'
And the little girl skipped home, smiling away!

Lucy Tolmie-Thomson (12)
St Mary's School, Shaftesbury

DEATH

He sinks to his knees.
Too fatigued to scream his pleas.
He wears a cloak of viscous mud,
And all he sees through blurry eyes is tainted blood.
His skin starts to ashen. His teeth start to chatter,
But none of this is what really matters.
Scarlet, warning him away,
But I'm afraid this will be his final day,
His crystal-blue eyes that knew the most,
Dispersed, and became his watching ghost.
As he gasps, and his soul is ready to fly,
He knows that in these moments he will die.
A single, lonely tear streaks down his face,
And it's in this moment that his mind starts to race.
Death isn't glorious. It isn't for the brave.
Death knows that we are all its slave.
Death is not heroic. It's more shocking than you know,
And just as the man drew his final breath,
No, there was no beautiful glow.

Megan Feltham (14)
St Mary's School, Shaftesbury

A PICTURE

A picture can say a thousand words they tell me,
A memory caught in a spiderweb, trapped and tucked away,
Once the click of a button has come.

I know this is true,
When I look at her,
She is whispering to me,
However quiet, however far,
She is always smiling, always there.

Something you can hold,
When the other is gone,
Something that feels the pitter-patter of tears,
Or the ringing sound of laughter.

Whenever I am lost for words,
I look at her and know that,
That memory under lock and key,
Will stay the same forever,
However much I change.

Tabitha Elwell (12)
St Mary's School, Shaftesbury

THE NIGHT TOWN

A dark abandoned alleyway,
Houses and shops,
Sirens soaring past
Along the concrete road.
The lights flickered like a burning candle,
Smoke rising from the dusted chimney,
All humans asleep,
All predators awake.
One girl running home
As her warm, scared tears run elegantly down her cold face,
As her heart shattered into a thousand pieces like a porcelain doll.

Sophie Levy
Stanchester Academy, Stoke-Sub-Hamdon

GLOBAL WARMING

The wolf stands alone, cubs thin, bony
Sickly, small, hunger gnawing at their bones
Gunshot rings in their ears
Killed one – three dead

Orang-utan sat at my feet
Beauty disappeared
Child gone to the next place
Soon to join her

Amazon? Where?
A forest was there?
I don't believe you!

Polar bears trapped
Under the ice
No way of escape
Heart stopping, breath slowing, mother missing.

Amur leopard, thirty-five left
Maybe less
Is that the last one?
No three! She has cubs

Tiger growl, tiger prowl
Hunting proudly in the night
Heart racing, 'Stop! Stop!'
Bang!

Black panther's beauty strong
His rosettes down his back
Leopard's cousin
One click of the trigger; gone.

Emma Thornton (12)
Stanchester Academy, Stoke-Sub-Hamdon

CITY OF SHADOWS

Everyone dead yet the city's alive,
Abandoned, isolated and crushed at heart,
Lifeless and broken the city's grand hall was dim in the dark,
Corpses hung from pointed spires oozing with blood,
Crows infested the lone city's core,
Heartless souls surround the beaten-down tree,
Lost, found, or gone,
Whistling wind and aching screams fill the air,
Smoke strangled the perished children,
Diseased and deadly roamed the drained fountain,
Twisted minds invade the streets,
Nothing but shadows built it,
Cold air coiled the walls and peaks of the mountains' edge,
Everyone dead yet the city's alive.

Indianna Alisha Collins (12)
Stanchester Academy, Stoke-Sub-Hamdon

HORROR NIGHT

Halloween is coming
But don't you fear
Halloween is coming
The streets filled with cheer
Halloween is coming
And I'll make this clear
Halloween is coming
Things lurking in the dark
Halloween is coming
Don't go near the park
Halloween is coming
The werewolves are out
Halloween is coming
Listen to them shout
Halloween is coming
Without a doubt
Halloween is coming
Time to dress up
Halloween is coming
Don't give up
Halloween is coming
Sweet bowls being filled
Halloween is coming
Tills are being filled
Halloween is here
But remember what I've told you
And I've made it clear.

Jade Orchard
Voyage Learning Campus – Weston, Oldmixon

LOVERS THAT CHANGED HISTORY

Love is supposed to be a peaceful thing.
Love is supposed to be about butterflies and rainbows.
But these two blood-loving lovers changed the word love for good.
Blood, sweat and tears.
A blood-shedding king longing for a new queen.
Religion, beliefs and views must change.
One woman, one man, with one desire
High council would never approve
But who would question?
Who would keep their head?
Who would disobey his request?
New churches, a new religion.
No one to object.
A king's wish for all to obey.
In the end it was all for nothing,
The king wanted a third wife and what a king wants a king will get.
Poor Anne Boleyn's head lay upon a long wooden stick
While happy Henry awaits his new wife.

Chloe-Jayne Britt
Voyage Learning Campus – Weston, Oldmixon

Young**Writers**
Est. 1991

YOUNG WRITERS INFORMATION

We hope you have enjoyed reading this book – and that you will continue to in the coming years.

If you're a young writer who enjoys reading and creative writing, or the parent of an enthusiastic poet or story writer, do visit our website www.youngwriters.co.uk. Here you will find free competitions, workshops and games, as well as recommended reads, a poetry glossary and our blog.

If you would like to order further copies of this book, or any of our other titles give us a call or visit **www.youngwriters.co.uk**.

Young Writers
Remus House
Coltsfoot Drive
Peterborough
PE2 9BF

(01733) 890066
info@youngwriters.co.uk